John P. Anderson, William Wallace

Life of Arthur Schopenhauer

John P. Anderson, William Wallace

Life of Arthur Schopenhauer

ISBN/EAN: 9783337731540

Printed in Europe, USA, Canada, Australia, Japan

Cover: Foto ©ninafisch / pixelio.de

More available books at **www.hansebooks.com**

"Great Writers."

EDITED BY

PROFESSOR ERIC S. ROBERTSON, M.A.

LIFE OF SCHOPENHAUER.

LIFE

OF

ARTHUR SCHOPENHAUER

BY

W. WALLACE,

WHYTE'S PROFESSOR OF MORAL PHILOSOPHY, OXFORD.

LONDON

WALTER SCOTT, 24 WARWICK LANE

1890

CONTENTS.

CHAPTER I.

The masters of philosophy in Germany have generally been the University professors; in England, members of the outside public; causes and effects, advantages and disadvantages of each of these circumstances; Schopenhauer more akin to the English than to the German philosopher; fundamental differences between his early training and that of his German predecessors; his contempt for the historical method in theology and philosophy; his definition of the true philosophy of history; the function of history merely accessary and illustrative; Schopenhauer gained an audience among the people because he helped to free the mind from historical paraphernalia 11

CHAPTER II.

Arthur Schopenhauer born at Dantzic, 22nd February, 1788; Dutch extraction; national characteristics inherited even on alien ground; inherits the Dutch mercantile pride; ancestors; father; mother; their home life; birth; early years; Dantzic merged in the Prussian kingdom; history of Dantzic; the Schopenhauers move to Hamburg, 1793; influence of the Dantzic republican spirit; an inverted education—experience preceding books; his father's view of a commercial education; goes to Havre, 1797; returns to Hamburg, 1799; school there; dislikes the prospects of a commercial life; declines the alternative offered by his father; starts with his parents on a tour through Europe, 1803 to 1805; three months at a Wimbledon boarding-school; early traits of character, and impressions of his journey; enters a merchant's office at Dantzic, 1804, and at Hamburg, 1805; attends Gall's lectures on mental physiology; death of his father, April, 1805; his mother goes to Weimar, and becomes a social and literary success; he comes under the influence of Romanticism; Romanticism defined; dissatisfaction with life; his mother agrees to his retiring from mercantile life; his gratitude to his father 22

CHAPTER III.

Development of classical studies—especially of Greek—in the early years of this century; Schopenhauer goes to school at Gotha and Weimar, 1807; his enthusiasm for the classics; his strained relations with his mother, due to their opposite characters; his personal property; enters University of Göttingen, October, 1809; the position of philosophy at the time; his views of Plato and Kant; life at Göttingen; meets Wieland; moves to University of Berlin, 1811; his contempt for the "university professor"; the charges of plagiarism made against him; the contrast between him and Fichte; on the rise of Prussia against Napoleon, he moves to Rudolstadt, 1813; takes his Doctor's degree at Jena; publishes as his Doctor's essay "A Philosophical Treatise on the Fourfold Root of the Principle of Sufficient Reason," 1813; its qualities and method; returns to Weimar; further and final disagreements with his mother; who was to blame? his views on the heredity of the Will and Intellect; Goethe's theory of Light; he seeks Schopenhauer's support; the latter moves to Dresden, 1814; his essay "On Vision and Colours" (published, 1816) . . 55

CHAPTER IV.

Schopenhauer's life at Dresden; his pessimism; his contempt for the lower, physical nature of man; his objections to materialism and spiritualism; his "necessary creed—'I

CONTENTS.

believe in a metaphysic'"; the gradual growth of his philosophy; his contention that we can attain the true philosophy only by art, not by science; his definition of the true philosophy and the true philosopher; his view of genius—how far correct; his chief reading in philosophy; difficulties with his publisher; "The World as Will and Idea," published, 1818; its reception; his own opinion of the work; his twofold character as man and as thinker . 85

CHAPTER V.

"The World as Will and Idea": it is the exposition, not of a system, but of a single idea; its style; not an academic discourse, but the gospel of a true life; Schopenhauer wages war against the materialistic philosophy of the scientists; the chief place in philosophy belongs, not to the intellect, but to the will—the system of feelings and desires; the "realities" of science being mere appearances (ideas), science can never give a final explanation of reality; the true philosophy connects ideas with reality, its fundamental principle being the identity in man between the perceived (material) body and the felt (immaterial) will; this principle discussed; its application to the universe at large; the Will as a metaphysical power; by his possession of intellect man has lost his original fellow-feeling with all things, but by it he can regain that unity of feeling; in the artistic genius this unity of feeling finds fullest expression; the function of art is to reveal this unity of existence; man's ignorance of this unity results in his selfish quest of happiness and consequent wrong-doing, which law can do no more than curb; it is the function of morality to purge the individual will of its egoism; the highest life is that of the man who, dead to the lust of life, has ascended from the natural to the Spiritual Will . . 113

CHAPTER VI.

Contemporary enthusiasm for Italy; Schopenhauer visits Italy, 1818; his life there; financial trouble; his characteristic conduct in the matter; becomes college lecturer at Berlin, but fails, 1820; jealous suspicions of his rivals; his ill-temper leads him into litigation with a sempstress; visit to Switzerland and Italy; settles his dispute with the sempstress; his coarse, passionate nature; his love affairs; his views on women and sexuality; efforts to gain popularity; proposes to translate Kant into English; other translations; moves to Frankfort on the appearance of cholera in Berlin, 1831 138

CHAPTER VII.

Re-opens correspondence with his mother and sister; moves to Mannheim, 1832; finally settles as a confirmed bachelor at Frankfort, 1833; his estimate of the relative advantages of youth and age; the defects of youth; philosophy his chief consolation; his life at Frankfort; his ideas on history and literature, and on the advantages of a classical education; his love of animals; his objections to newspapers; publishes "On the Will in Nature," 1836; its method; he is still unappreciated; gains prize for an essay on the freedom of the Will, 1838; but another essay on the basis of morality is rejected; his consequent rage and general impatience of all rivalry or opposition, or even of silence concerning his works; discussion of his two essays, published in 1841 as "The Two Fundamental Problems of Ethics"; second edition of "The World as Will and Idea," 1844; his work at length appreciated, partly in consequence of the growth of historical criticism, scientific materialism, and democracy, with all of which he had no sympathy; insurrection in Frankfort, 1848; the chief of his early disciples; discussion of his "Parerga and Paralipomena" (published, 1851); his craving for public applause; the main body of his adherents drawn from the general public, to whom the many points dealt with in his philosophy, as well as his style and method, appealed; portraits of him; further grounds for dissatisfaction with the Universities; his solitary life and mode of living at Frankfort during his later years; his death, 21st September, 1860 165

INDEX 213

PREFATORY NOTE.

ANY Life of Schopenhauer must be founded on the biographical materials supplied by Gwinner and Frauenstädt. Besides these main sources, the following sketch has drawn from supplementary papers by his friends, has borrowed some descriptive notes from his mother, and has freely used the *Works*, especially the "Parerga and Paralipomena," to interpret the incidents of a somewhat uneventful life. It has thus sought to escape from the judgment of Schopenhauer, that "those who, instead of studying the thoughts of a philosopher, make themselves acquainted with his life and history, are like people who, instead of occupying themselves with a picture, are rather occupied with its frame, reflecting on the taste of its carving, and the nature of its gilding." But, after all, there is nothing to keep the English reader from using the ample resources recent translations have given him for getting at these thoughts more directly.

SCHOPENHAUER.

CHAPTER I.

PHILOSOPHERS in Germany take a different place in the literary commonwealth from what they hold among ourselves. With a few striking exceptions, it may be said that in England, down at least to the present day, the fountain head of the philosophical stream has not been in the Universities, and the professional element has been entirely secondary. In Germany, on the contrary, the treasures of learned wisdom have been entrusted to the keeping of a chosen official order, the teachers in the Universities.

It would be going out of the way to inquire into the ulterior causes of this circumstance, or to point out how it hangs together with more general contrasts in the social and political system of the two countries. Nor is it possible here to discuss at length the profit and loss which accrue according as the ideal interests of a community in science, art, or religion, are administered under a more or less direct delegation from the supreme power in the state, or left to the energy, enterprise, and good-will of private agencies. Yet it is clear that much depends on which arrangement is adopted. Without the guiding control of an academic system, there is apt to be waste and misdirection of effort, there is a risk of incoherence and inequality in the line of development, a tendency to eccentricity. But, in compensation, the self-taught and independent thinker is freed from the dangers of conventionalism, and he deals with the great problems of life and thought, not because it is his official duty to say something on them, but because his own reflections have made him realize difficulties, and seek for solutions of his difficulties.

On the other hand, German philosophy has had for some centuries a continuous tradition, a more or less uniform vocabulary and usage, which secures a tolerably high level of thinking even for mediocre minds, and to superior minds gives a discipline which guards against many an extravagance. Hence, on the whole, a more exact style of thought, a subtler power of logical analysis. But these gains are counterbalanced. Philosophy in Germany has, it is sometimes said, come to be something solely written by professors for professors, or for those who hope to be professors one day. In his anxiety to win the applause of his brother-experts, the writer has been accused of losing touch with the general public and the common sense of the nation. A narrower range of clients, with more technical knowledge, but also more liable to prejudice and conventional appreciations, may no doubt give its suffrages more reasonably, yet the specialist, even the philosophical specialist, is apt to lose the true sense of proportions, and his approbation cannot make up for the absence of that popular sympathy and interest which is as indispensable to the health of philosophy, art, and religion, as it is for the harmonious movement of the political system.

And again, just because the utterances of philosophy in Germany have been chiefly made through an established and endowed order, it has been largely bound up with the interests of theology and sobered by its connection with the general machinery of the state. In the inevitable give and take, it is true, theology has gained an ampler and opener spirit, and philosophy has dared to deal with higher questions, than either could hope for in England. Turned into an engine for the preparation of youth, philosophy must surely gain traits of conservatism, and put on magisterial vestments which embarrass its movements; while, on the other hand, it has helped to heighten the general faculty for practical administration by imbuing it with ideal elements. But in England—with some exceptions—and still more in France—philosophy has been in its main currents the mouthpiece of an opposition to the established order of beliefs—of a class, or of isolated individuals, recalcitrant to that orthodox philosophy, which is entrenched (though not under the name of philosophy) in the great ecclesiastical institutions of the country. The term "philosopher," and still more "philosophe," has been associated with a tendency to free-thinking, infidelity, and radical antagonism to all things established. Perhaps, in the impatience of mere authority, philosophy has occasionally behaved like an untamed Pegasus, flying wildly heavenward or elsewhere, as the fit might take it. At times, as in Hobbes and Bentham, it has been bumptious and obstinate; as in Locke, it has had a dangerous affinity for commonplace; and as in Hume, it has seemed scarcely conscious of the gravity of the issues. But, on the other hand, English philosophy has rarely forgotten its intimate kindred with the great mother of all higher speculation—with that crude and imperfectly organized substratum of popular opinion, out of which it perpetually springs, and to give a clear and distinct re-organization to which must always be its main concern. While German philosophy has used a technical dialect of its own, English philosophy has been written in the ordinary language of literature. If it does not always reach the dignified eloquence it wields in Bacon and Mill, or even Hobbes, it still commands attention by its honest simplicity in Locke, and its vigorous debating power in Bentham. It is otherwise in Germany. There are, it is true, in Kant, as there are in his great successors, passages which have the power that true and adequate words always have to reach even the popular intellect: but, in large part, these writers are to their countrymen a book with seven seals. They are believed, not always without ground, to have held it enough if they knew what they were saying, without taking the further trouble of saying it intelligibly to others. So inexplicable has been their obscurity, that the vulgar have explained it as wilful mystification.

In many of these points Schopenhauer reminds of England more than of Germany. It was indeed only after a lingering struggle that he reluctantly abandoned all hopes of a University post, and took his place among the free-lances of speculation. If it had been possible, he would have been glad to enter the regular army of philosophic teachers, and work according to its regulations. But there was other work for him to do. He was to become an Apostle to the Gentiles, to the uncircumcised heathen, now that the chosen people of culture and learning had refused to hear him. For the work of a systematic teacher he was without the requisite preparation of methodical training, and still more wanting in the regular, precise, and almost prosaic faculty which metes out wisdom in palpable bulks for consumption by audiences, drawn not primarily by philosophic passion, but by the pressure of academic ordinances. But if he was unsuited to be a teacher of that systematic logic and ethics in which he had never been a thorough learner, he was by his very dilettantism, by his literary faculty, by his interest in problems as they strike the natural mind, qualified to stimulate, to guide, perhaps even to fascinate, those who like himself were led by temperament, by situation, by inward troubles, to ask the why and the wherefore of all this unintelligible world.

He came to his work with other training and prepossessions than the majority of his philosophical rivals or predecessors. In the long list of the more notable teachers of Germany, from Christian Wolff in the end of the seventeeth to Hegel in the end of the eighteenth century, most had, as children of peasants, or artisans, or humble officials, to toil through the dull and steep approaches of tutorial or other drudgery till they received the pittance awarded to the state-paid teachers of philosophy. Instead of the tight and heavy yoke they had to wear, Schopenhauer, after he had picked up easy lessons in the open book of the natural and the social world, was, in the years of opening manhood, with income enough to steer an independent way, left free to form and expound his convictions on the purpose of life and the worth of the universe. It was not altogether gain indeed : his liberty was as the independence of a voice crying in the wilderness : the unlicensed teacher was unregarded ; and the official philosophers, if they did not, as he wildly supposed, conspire to ignore him, yet acted on the feeling that it was scarcely within their strict duty to examine into the pretensions of this unaccredited missionary.

As little had he imbibed much of the historical beliefs, especially in religion, under which their youth had been led. Hence he had to go through hardly any of that disburthening and remodelling by which the great thinkers of his earlier time had sought to transmute into their permanent value, or ideal significance, the theological creeds they had inherited. From Kant to Hegel the theological prepossession dominates their inward reflections. Almost the last work of Kant is to square accounts between his all-unhinging criticism and the religious dogmas of his Evangelical teachers, whose intrinsic truth he still assumes. Fichte begins his career by a criticism of revelation in general. Schelling's first literary performance is a college essay on the philosophical value of the old religious legends, and his latest studies are embodied in his lectures on the philosophy of mythology and the philosophy of revelation. Hegel, in hours of leisure during his Swiss tutorship, works out for himself the inner and everlasting purport of the Gospel story; and only two summers before his death he was lecturing on what are called the "Proofs" for the existence of God.

Of all this reconciliatory work Schopenhauer spared himself the trouble. His upbringing had made religion lie very much outside him—a formal thing, which had never appropriated his whole soul. He had not gone through the inward contests of faith: and came to philosophy with only the minimum of an inherited and adopted creed. Hence to him these efforts at reconciliation seemed hypocritical:—as they may naturally do to those who have not grown up under historic influences, or who have not learned how dependent the individual intellect, even the greatest, is on the great historic tradition of faith and knowledge. Hence it was easy and natural for Schopenhauer to pass by Christian theology and modern Christianity with a sniff of contempt, and to groan out the words *Foetor Judaicus!* With a great deal in the asceticism and pessimism of early Christianity he was thoroughly in sympathy. But its deep sense of the evil in the world, and of the need of self-renunciation, had been obscured, he thought, through the re-actionary influence of the national optimism and the old legendary superstitions of the Hebrews. It was for these reasons that he turned admiringly to the less historically-coloured religion of Buddha, with its more purely human scheme of salvation. It was not that he rejected miracle as such. What he rejected was the limitation of miracles to a few years of the world's history, to a special interposition, an extra-mundane design. On the contrary, he taught the eternal presence of the miraculous in life and nature,—the presence in all things of a supreme reality, which never ceased from evincing itself superior to the law of causality, and the limitations of space and time. For him, therefore, Christianity erred by laying stress on the historical accuracy of a record of event, by limiting to one place and person the process of redemption, instead of seeing that its truths were for all time, and told of the universe. Not otherwise had the philosophers taught from whom he so bitterly disagreed. Only, while they had accentuated the inner harmony between philosophy and religion, he had no eyes except for the outward discordance between the attitude of faith and the attitude of reflection.

The antithesis was part of a settled contempt for the purely historical which marks Schopenhauer. To such a turn of mind the contrast between science and history, which all philosophy teaches, was exaggerated to thorough depreciation of the latter. His contemporaries, not least Hegel, were engaged in an attempt to get at the meaning of present reality by means of a historical method; they sought to show that the slow process of history is, under the form of time, a gradual revelation of the organic principles which form the basis of actual life. The condensed and opaque reality of the present (they held) becomes transparent, and unfolds its inner structure and stratification, only to one who has watched step by step the successive concretion of its members along the course of history. Thus they adopted, but subordinated, the historical method, as an organon for philosophical inquiry. Schopenhauer will hardly allow it any value at all. The penetrative imagination of genius, *i.e.*, of the philosopher as he conceives him, could at a single glance see farther and deeper than the duller eye of the mere scholar could hope to range, even with all the optical helps of erudition and archæology. The so-called progress disclosed by history is, in his judgment, only a delusion, due to laying unmerited emphasis on certain accidents of scenery, drapery, and outward figure. "The true philosophy of history," he says (with latent reference to contemporary attempts to construct the scheme of historical advance), " lies in perceiving that, in all the endless changes and motley complexity of event, it is only the self-same unchangeable being which is before us, which to-day pursues the same ends as it did yesterday and as it ever will. The historical philosopher has accordingly to recognize the identical character in all events, of the ancient and the modern world, of the East and the West ; and in spite of all the variety of special circumstances, of costume, and of manners and customs, has to see everywhere the same humanity. This self-same element, which persists through all change, consists in the fundamental qualities of heart and head—many bad, a few good. The motto of philosophy in general must run : *Eadem sed aliter.* To have read Herodotus is, from a philosophical point of view, to have studied enough history. For in him you already find everything that makes subsequent history—the acts and pursuits, the life and destiny of the human race, as they flow from the aforesaid qualities in conjunction with physical conditions."

It would be ungrateful to disparage the value of historical research, and betray a doctrinaire hardness to resist its charms. But it would be worse than ungrateful to fail to resist the mere impulse of curiosity, and to take the pathos and glamour of incident for the light of reason. History, in the strict sense, is but a handmaid to science and philosophy: her function accessary and illustrative. The so-called historical method but serves to correct the mistakes into which the mere analysis of conceptions may fall when conducted apart from the real presence of fact; it corrects bare theory by the observation of the actual operation of ideas in the world, but can only conduct that observation by help of the premature and fallible theory it assumes. The lessons of history, like those of experience in general, are only apprehended and estimated at their due value by those who already have a general grasp of the truth which these lessons are supposed to enforce. For these reasons one may excuse the exaggeration in which Schopenhauer helps to free the mind from its perpetual antiquarianism—its tendency to worship the mere historical, and to count the ancient swaddling-clothes of a truth worth preserving, as a sort of guarantee that the truth has not been stolen or lost. It is antiquarianism—the extravagance of intellectual relic-worship—which Schopenhauer censures. There is for many good people a picturesque pathos in these old vestments; but the truth is not in the museums and sepulchres where they lie: it "is risen."

The charm of the historical is owned by those who can identify themselves and their faith with the past. It is natural to the classes who inherit their position, their aims, their duties; who are bound by links of love, and custom, and obedience, to the generations that have gone before. But to the rebel and the revolutionary, to the heterodox and the isolated, to the new workers and thinkers, who have to stand for themselves—for that vast multitude in the modern world which is continually drifting or being driven from its ancient moorings —the historical can never be the one thing needful. Schopenhauer gained an audience amongst those thus disinherited (by their own or others' act) of their ancestral goods, spiritual or natural, because he cast away all those paraphernalia of philological and historical erudition which the cultured scholarly mind is liable to rank as the very heart of the matter. People felt that here was one who spoke directly to their needs, and who was no mere "scribe" expounding a dogma which he had been hired to defend, and which stood on the borrowed authority of its historical lineage. One may be sorry that such a division between the scholar and the mass of the populace should exist. But it is unfortunately the fact that this interposition of historical form and material is what cuts off a great majority of the world from any direct access to truth. It is what renders nine out of every ten sermons so inefficacious, because really meaningless, to their hearers. That historical partition-wall Schopenhauer does not entirely break through; but, at least, he is less encompassed and hampered by it than most of his rivals. Hence his success in quarters where philosophy rarely makes its name heard, still less its influence felt.

CHAPTER II.

ARTHUR SCHOPENHAUER was born at Dantzic on February 22, 1788.

Through both parents he could claim Dutch extraction. Among these ancestors the traditions of his family had especially preserved the memory of a great-grandfather of his mother, who had held some ecclesiastical post at Gorcum (or Gorinchem) in Holland, and that memory was still fresh enough to take young Schopenhauer with his parents out of their way to visit the spot where their forefather had preached. Three generations backward from 1788 would take us near the time when Spinoza died (February 21, 1677). And it is not without a quaint pathological interest we hear that Schopenhauer, who prided himself on his intellectual kindred to the great Jew, had thought so much on these dates as to note it down, for an odd coincidence, that he was ushered into the world exactly 111 years and one day after Spinoza left it.

Perhaps the influence of his Dutch lineage has more importance than these fancies of a strange transmigration of souls through cycles of time. It is no doubt easy to fall into fantastic analogies in the attempt to trace the evidence for a persistence of national characteristics in those who have been long since parted from their ancestral soil. But it is only a cheap scepticism which chooses to ignore an influence altogether, because it lurks in obscurity and refuses to be accurately estimated. The organic memories of race and family linger, still effective, amid new environments. The biographers of St. Francis of Assisi, struck by his passionate sympathy with all creatures of field and wood, and by his glowing strain of poetry, have sometimes gone so far as to seek the explanation, not in mere associations with Provence, but in the hypothesis of his mother belonging to that land of France, from which he got his name. Others have found a significance in the fact that the father of the light-hearted Boccaccio had taken a wife from the daughters of Paris. And similar instances of the way hereditary characters prevail on alien ground are seen in the history of philosophers. Stoicism and the later sects of Greek wisdom owe some of their tone and shading to the Oriental blood which ran in the veins of many of their adherents. And, coming to later times, it is hardly possible to help seeing in the caution, the dry humour, the blending of coolness and fervour, in Kant, the symptoms of his Scotch ancestry.

And from the latter philosopher, who was an eager student of geography and anthropology, and had many opportunities of observing national types in the mixed society of his native town, we can gather some idea of what effects the Dutch mercantile lineage might leave behind. The commercial spirit, remarks Kant, has a general similarity to the temper of aristocracy everywhere.

It is essentially unsocial. "One house—as the merchant calls his office—is parted from another by its business engagements, as thoroughly as one feudal castle from another by its drawbridge, and all friendly intercourse, free from ceremony, is proscribed." But the Dutch capitalist has his peculiar phase of mercantile pride. While the Englishman says "The man is worth a million," and the Frenchman, "He possesses a million," the merchant of Holland looks up to one who "commands a million." And Dutch pride in general is marked off from other forms by its insolent contempt for others, by a puffed-up conceit which is regardless of other's feelings and ready to lapse into rudeness. So far Kant. It will be seen that Schopenhauer too often justifies this prognosis.

But, whatever weight may be due to the transmission of moral types, these ancestors from the Netherlands had for two or three generations lain open to all the social and political influences of Dantzic, where they had settled in the course of commerce. At the beginning of the eighteenth century, Andreas Schopenhauer, the great-grandfather of the subject of this narrative, was lessee of one of the large farms belonging to the municipality, combining, as many have done, the business of the merchant with the calmer interests of the rural cultivator. His son, another Andreas, pursued the same family career, blending mercantile with landed pursuits. He had acquired a piece of property at Ohra, a southern suburb of Dantzic; and there in his house, amid an ample garden, he retired to spend his declining days. On the same spot, after his death in 1794, his widow continued to reside for a few years longer—but under guardianship, since she was deemed hardly fit to manage her own affairs. From her the children of this Andreas seem to have inherited in various degrees some congenital weakness or perturbation of spirit. The eldest son, also called Andreas (who died in 1816) was from his youth upwards imbecile. The second son, who died in 1795, left behind him a character for foolish and discreditable prodigality. The youngest of the family—and father of the philosopher—was Heinrich Floris, born in 1747.

Henry Schopenhauer seems to have received all the intelligence and perseverance which had been denied to some of his brothers. In conjunction with another brother, John Frederick, who died young, he created for their firm a character for enterprise and success which was second to none among the merchant houses of the old Hanse town. The dominant feature of his nature was a resolute tenacity of purpose, a passion for independence and distinction, which sought more than mercantile gain. He was conspicuous in the city for his knowledge of affairs, a cosmopolitan habit of mind, and a reputation for what may be styled "advanced" or "enlightened" views. In his judgments on the deeper problems of human life he was a disciple of the school of Voltaire. He was well-read in the lighter—which then was also often the more frivolous and non-moral literature—of France and England. His tastes were such as beseem the ambitions of the cavalier and the aristocrat— such as fired the merchant princes in Italian republics. This superficial culture was unequally matched with his bodily endowments. A square and muscular frame, broad face with wide mouth and prominent underjaw, did not give him precisely the look of an Adonis; but they sufficiently indicated a surplus of vitality and self-assertion, and a robust power little tempered by delicacy, grace, or sympathy. A physical hardness of hearing helped to intensify the spirit of isolation, and would easily lead into what seemed obstinacy and severity.

In her maiden days the mother of Arthur Schopenhauer was known by the name of Johanna Henriette Trosiener. She too was born and nurtured in one of the families which managed the policy of Dantzic. Her father, a member of the City Council, was one of the party which wanted to adapt the constitution to supposed modern requirements, whereas Heinrich Schopenhauer had more faith in the capacity of the old patrician system to ride safely through the storms of the time. Like his future son-in-law too he was a man who had travelled widely, and had acquired a relish for those literary and artistic adornments of life in which Dantzic was still somewhat lacking. Unfortunately he resembled him no less in vehemency of temper. When these fits of fury fell upon him, his children would cower before the storm; but his wife let the empty turbulence roll past her undisturbed. It was after her that Johanna took: an easy life-enjoying disposition, a quick observant eye, and a deft artistic hand; a neat figure (at least in early life) with clear blue eyes and light brown hair; graceful and charming rather than pretty; always a little conscious of her own advantages, and liable to self-complacency. Her education had been laid out on broader lines than usually prescribed the training assigned to young maidens in Dantzic or elsewhere at that date. In her early years the fair Johanna attracted the notice of her father's neighbour in town, Dr. Jameson, an Edinburgh minister, who looked after the spiritual needs of the British colony there. Under his friendly lead her reading was ampler in range, and more stimulating in quality, than could be expected from the cut-and-dried themes of the school-room. Unfortunately this sympathetic mentor was withdrawn from her about the time of her marriage: the Scottish clergyman was obliged, perhaps in consequence of the commercial depression of the time, to quit Dantzic for his native land. But Johanna had also a special tutor of her own—a kind of youthful "Dominie Sampson," whose susceptible breast was so smitten by her charms that one day, when she was just thirteen, she was startled by his open avowal of his love. The unwelcome suitor was soon disposed of, but we do not wonder that at the age of eighteen years (she was born in 1766) this winsome young lady attracted the attention and admiration of Heinrich Schopenhauer, who was then thirty-eight. The prospective bridegroom certainly was far from handsome; but an ugly face was counterbalanced by a prominent position in the city, a reputation for ability and courage, and the prestige of a well-appointed establishment, not to mention an evidently strong and genuine devotion of love. Anyhow she did not keep her wooer long waiting for a favourable reply, and without professing for him an attachment which she scarcely felt, she consented to become his wife. After a very short engagement, they were married, May 16, 1785—heedless, if aware, of the penalties which vulgar faith has in many regions assigned to wedlock initiated in the month of May.

The young wife took up her abode in her husband's country house. About four miles to the north-west of Dantzic, a little south of the main road which runs from Striess to Oliva, there stood a few villas belonging to the Dantzic merchants, who then, as now, sought release in summer from the heat and noise of their busy town. Behind these villas rises a prettily-wooded range of low sand-hills, looking forth on the Baltic, and forming the outlying bulwark of that undulating range of forest which covers the inland regions of Pomerellen. One of these country-seats, towards Oliva, was the summer home of Schopenhauer. It was, however, only from a Saturday to a Monday that the master of the house came out to spend with his wife the few leisure hours he allowed himself from his desk. Even then too he generally brought with him a friend or two from town, and on Sunday a number of other guests sat round their table. Only once could his wife remember a visit from her husband in the course of the week, and that was when one day—even though it was a specially busy time,—he rode out from town to announce the fall of the Bastille. But except on a rare occasion like this, Johanna had the solitary enjoyment of what treasures and pleasures the villa might offer. Within were prints and casts of classic and noted works of art, and a well-stored library of French and English literature, especially strong in novels: without was a terraced garden with ancient elms and beeches, a pond with a boat light enough for one person to manage—were spaniels, eight pet-lambs (the several bells of which rung an octave as they gambolled together), and a pair of horses in the stables: while two or three miles away, in perpetual variety from day to day and hour to hour, lay or tossed the East Sea between the mole of Dantzic haven at Neufahrwasser on the east, and the long promontory of sandy woodland which curves round from the west to terminate in the lighthouse at Hela.

In such scenes, varied by a removal to town when the winter set in, and by occasional visits to her parental home, Johanna passed the two first years of wedded life —a prisoner of love, for whom the ease of this *dolce far niente* was pierced by occasional longings for an ampler life and a more definite sphere of action. So too it continued even after her first child was born. And yet it was what may be called an accident that her son Arthur first saw light in No. 117 of the Heiligengeist Strasse at Dantzic in 1788. In the midsummer of the preceding year the married couple started on the first of those tours which ere long became a habitual feature of their life. The intention of Schopenhauer, who, like so many a continental in the eighteenth century, regarded England as a promised land of liberty and intelligence, was that his expected child should be born on English soil, and appropriate what profits accrue to those so indigenous. But, so far as such purpose existed, it failed; and its failure was the first misfortune which, as one may say, crossed the path of the philosopher. For, after travelling by Pyrmont, Frankfort, and Paris, they had reached London, and spent some weeks there, a sudden fit of home sickness on the part of the young wife led to a precipitate return to Dantzic, across Northern Germany, in the depth of winter. The child thus perversely ushered into the world as a native of Germany, in one of the gabled houses of the old Hanse town, was baptized in the Marienkirche on the 3rd of March, by the name of Arthur—a choice, it is told, prompted by the father's wish to endow the future chief of the firm with a truly cosmopolitan Christian name. Young Arthur grew up for the next five years, as other children do, his mother's idol and delight. In the very year of his birth, the Stuthof—the meadow farm held more than half a century before by Andreas Schopenhauer—had fallen vacant, and Johanna's father took the opportunity of renting the estate, with a view of getting a change of scene and air for his children, and providing an easy occupation for his own advancing years. The farm—adjacent to a village of the same name—lay at the very eastern limit of the Dantzic territory, enclosed between the Baltic Sea and the arms of the Vistula. The most delightful feature of the spot was a fragrant pine-wood covering the sandy downs (*dünen*) by the sea, and visitors to it long remembered the sweet notes of the tinkling cow-bells as the herd pastured in those fresh sunny days when spring at last bursts out in these landscapes with wreaths of verdure and flowers. To the Stuthof every May Johanna would rush off with her child to spend the month, while her husband was too burdened with business cares to find time for his weekly visit to Oliva. Relics of old times and ways still hung about the manor. There could be seen an interesting memorial of feudal customs—the days when the dependent peasantry were obliged to perform their covenanted dole of work for the lord of the manor in presence of the bailiff with his whip. An old servant of the place still remembered the time of Andreas Schopenhauer, and was fond of telling the visitor how that worthy had covered himself with glory on the occasion of the Czar Peter's sojourn there in 1718. For when the great Czar and his spouse Catherine had honoured him by electing to spend the night in one of his chambers, which was stoveless, their host had promptly solved the problem of heating it, by setting fire to some gallons of brandy which had been emptied on the stone floor, and thus diffusing through the room a vapour of spirituous warmth most acceptable to the imperial couple.

The child meanwhile found the life of the farmsteading full of pleasant surprises. He was caught one day standing in front of a large vessel full of milk, making request to a shoe which he had tossed in to jump out again. The incident, which stuck to his memory, led him to make in his early MS. the following sententious remarks: "The child has no conception of the inexorableness of natural law, and of the rigidity with which everything sticks to its own nature. He believes that even inanimate things will give way to him a little; perhaps because he feels himself one with nature, perhaps because, unacquainted with the real essence of the world, he believes it his friend. . . . It is a still later experience which teaches that human characters too are inflexible, and shows us that no entreaty, or representation, or example, or kindness can make them depart from their course; but how, on the contrary, each must enact his special mode of conduct, character, and capacity, with the inevitableness of a law of nature."

Meanwhile the last act of a long political struggle was rushing to its close around the unconscious heads of mother and child. Dantzic—to which its admirers give the proud title of the "Venice of the North"—was fast being encircled by the rising power of Prussia and writhed in impotent rage against the inevitable doom of absorption. It is difficult at the present day realize the vivid force of the principle of republican autonomy which animated the "free towns," and the depth of their dislike to the autocratic principalities which confronted them. For the upper orders in such a community the sense of citizenship was a proud possession, which they would not have exchanged for any post of dignified servility at the court of prince or king. The successive steps in the growth of the Prussian monarchy were so many grades in the process which curtailed these privileges. And men like Henry Schopenhauer—with his added tradition of Dutch freedom—felt acutely the contrast between the old virtual independence and absorption into what then seemed a mere military despotism of a low and mechanical type. We cannot then, wonder that the issue of the struggle touched their feelings deeply. Theoretically Dantzic was a part of the Polish kingdom, and her allegiance lay outside Germany. Practically it was a state by itself. The history of Dantzic had its charms for her patriotic citizens. They could go back to the fourteenth century when, after early struggles with the Polish tribes around them, they had become subject to the great Teutonic Order, which sought to fortify the faith and convert the heathen on these then half-savage plains. But the glory and the strength of Dantzic came from her partnership in the Hanseatic League, and as her citizens grew potent and wealthy they could ill brook the domination of the now decaying Order. In 1454 they had thrown off the yoke and destroyed the castle of the Knights, and, through the process of a twelve years' warfare, succeeded in winning virtual independence, subject to the undefined and rarely exerted suzerainty of the kings of Poland. The sixteenth century, after the revolt of the Netherlands had closed against the Dutch the Catholic ports in the South, was the most prosperous age in Dantzic's history. Its trade—consisting chiefly in grain which descended the river in barges manned by Polish crews—extended as far as Spain and Italy; and a counter current of exchange in the shape of ideas and arts flowed in from the southern ports. The houses and churches of Dantzic bear a traceable witness to the example of the Italian renaissance; one of its gates imitates Sammichele's work at Verona; and the able youth of the city were encouraged, even by "bursaries" or "exhibitions," to seek at the University of Padua that legal knowledge which, like the *jus civile* in senatorial Rome, was held the most needful and also the most honourable study in the commercial republic. To Dantzic, however, as to the rest of Germany, the seventeeth century brought the calamities of the Thirty Years' War; it brought also, and especially, a succession of intestine feuds, of border raids waged by ambitious and turbulent adventurers, and it increased the violence of the contrasts between rapacious wealth and a discontented populace. The government was passing more and more into the hands of a clique; and the mass of the people, excluded from the spoils of office, freely accused the ruling class of dishonesty and nepotism. In 1734 the city, in consequence of having given a refuge within its walls to Stanislaus Leczinski, the French candidate for the crown of Poland, was subjected to a fierce five months' siege by the Russian forces, which ended in its capitulation, and involved the payment of a heavy pecuniary indemnity to the victors.

The catastrophe of Poland was also the downfall of independence for Dantzic. In that fall there were several stages. In 1772 came off the first of those national crimes known as the partitions of Poland. By that arrangement, which assigned to Prussia all the rest of the Polish districts to the west of the Lower Vistula, Dantzic was left to a nominal autonomy. But Frederick the Great was dissatisfied with these conditions, which the jealousy of Russia and other powers had imposed upon him. The possession of Dantzic was essential to the commercial unity of his kingdom. He proceeded accordingly from his stations in the vicinity—he was master of the fort at Weichselmünde by the harbour, as well as of the inland regions—to make the place too hot for its inhabitants. A customs barrier so completely invested the town on all sides of approach that the patricians, when they would pay a visit to their suburban seats at Oliva, or even at Langefuhr, just outside the gates, had to submit to what they considered the insolence, and, it might be, the exactions, of the custom-house officials curiously inquiring into the wine and provisions they brought out with them. Even the mere formalities of the *douane*, managed by French *employés*, could be exasperating enough, when practised in such minutiæ. The City Council, aware of the dangers of the situation, made attempts at compromise with Prussia; but their efforts were foiled by the ignorant cries of treason that proceeded from the lower ranks of the populace. While this conflict in tariffs was going on, Heinrich Schopenhauer, who in the spring of 1773 was on his way home after a long absence in foreign parts, had an interview with the Prussian king at Potsdam. Conversation naturally turned to the question of the practically blockaded city. The king urged the merchant to settle in Prussia, and though his arguments were ineffectual on a man whose motto was *Point de bonheur sans liberté*, he sent the republican a formal license permitting him to take up an unhampered settlement on any part of Prussian territory. Thus for several years this vexatious surveillance continued to harass the life and to destroy the trade of Dantzic, at least of those parts of it which were still outside Prussian rule. On one of these occasions, as late as 1784, the commander of the investing troops, who had his quarters in the house of old Andreas Schopenhauer, at Ohra, offered to show his sense of his entertainer's kindness by permitting forage to pass through the lines for the fine stud of horses for which his host's son Heinrich was famous. "'Tell the commander," replied the latter, when the offer was brought to his notice, "that my stores are full, and when they fail, my horses will be killed."

On the death of Frederick the Great in 1786, the more

thoughtless of the Dantzic citizens rejoiced as if all peril were over. But wiser heads judged otherwise. If the German arms gained no great glory in their campaigns against revolutionary France, they were at least strong enough to give the final quietus to the republican irregularities of Dantzic. In accordance with the programme of the second partition of Poland, a Prussian corps, on the 8th of March, 1793, arrived in front of the city to consummate the annexation; and after a few weeks' delay, accorded by the general in order to assuage the rage of the betrayed people, Dantzic ceased to exist as a "free city." The Schopenhauers did not wait for the end. As soon as the enemy appeared, Heinrich determined to depart; with wife and child he started in the night for his country house, and next day proceeded in haste through Pomerania on the road to Hamburg. This transference of domicile was a costly affair, involving not merely the natural loss from a hasty forced realization of capital, but the further penalty of a duty of 10 per cent. payable to the fiscal authorities by the candidate for expropriation.

Thus at the age of five, Schopenhauer followed his parents into exile. Though they settled at Hamburg, and though the father carried on his business there for the next twelve years, he never became a naturalized citizen. Something was broken in the proud spirit. He refused to set foot in Dantzic again, and only allowed his wife a visit to her relatives every few years. Yet the influence of the commercial republic was a paramount element in determining the character both of father and son. Like all such influences it has its good and its evil. Its good is a fearlessness and audacity of view, an independence of judgment, a plain straightforwardness and simplicity of purpose. On the other side, republicanism on such a scale is apt to be proud and ill-disciplined, to breed an anarchic temper unfitted to work in regular harness or do its part in conjoint labour. The heads of great firms easily fall into an overbearing, dictatorial, and egotistic frame of mind. The whole city, with its oligarchical constitution, feels the want of the civilizing effect of regular authority put in the hands of one too high to be a mere despot. Lawlessness of spirit, working amid the trammels of an artificial legal system, encourages the formation of untamed characters who are more anxious to secure their rights than careful to consider their duties. A certain coarseness and hardness accompanies the purely mercantile life. As an indication of the temper of the place, it may be noted that a savage breed of dogs was kept to guard the great granaries on the Granary Island, though many tales were on record of unfortunate boatmen from the corn barges who, without any mischievous intent, had taken refuge in these sheds and been torn to pieces by their canine guardians. Many of the traits of the physical and mental fibre of such a city re-appear in Schopenhauer. Out of a family and a city of bankers and traders, whose chief intellectual pursuit is law, and whose culture goes little beyond a superficial polish of art and letters, he is the first scion who emerges into the higher ranges of intellectual life. In such a transference of force from one sphere to another, there will inevitably be a certain uncouthness in the new phase, but there will also be unquestionable vigour, honesty, and even a grand originality. The new force is fresh, spontaneous, and unhackneyed; is more heart-whole, less dissipated by collateral aims and secondary considerations.

The years which young Schopenhauer spent at Hamburg (1793-1807) form a second factor in the development of his mind and nature, which is not less pregnant of consequences than the environment of his infancy. They are the years of his first education, and that an education of a thoroughly peculiar type. For most young people of his position in life the period between their fifth and twentieth year is passed in regular discipline under uniform and artificial conditions. The learner is rarely left to himself, either at school or at home, but by a number of tasks methodically arranged is familiarized with the application of certain general principles to a matter selected and prepared beforehand. Books and verbal instruction generally are the staple instruments employed. Direct contact with the world of experience is, on the whole, avoided. The pupils move in an abstract and almost fictitious world; and are thus prepared in a large and 'liberal' way for the real world from which, as confusing and probably wicked, they are carefully kept apart. Their minds are made familiar with rules and principles, with formulæ and commandments, which they are encouraged to embody and apply in a body of selected instances. Amongst other things, a scheme of moral and religious precepts is presented to them, on which, as they are encouraged to believe, the complex details of actual life are solidly established. The world they deal with is a world simplified, reduced to what the wisdom of ages has agreed to recognize as its essential reality. It was through a career like this that Schopenhauer's contemporaries approached life—they saw it through the medium of books, of general categories, and of historical forms. Their reasoning powers had been developed on comparatively abstract subjects. In the case of Schopenhauer, the faculties of perception, of observation, of judgment, in dealing with the raw material of life, were the first to be exercised. His training was fragmentary and spasmodic, and he only went to school and college after he had accomplished his grand tour of Europe, instead of, as others do, before it. Yet the difference need not be exaggerated, and either course has its peculiar perils. If the ordinary pupil is liable to overestimate forms and words and reasoning, the exceptional career of one who is left more freely to his own devices, and who only borrows a little from many casual masters, is apt to foster its peculiar fallacies. If it gives a vivid and picturesque reality to thoughts, clothing abstract ideas in their real instances, it often causes laxity in the hold of principles, and mistakes an illustration for an argument. There is danger in the study of mere words, no doubt; but, after all, words are the very body and reality of thought, and not to understand their uses and limits is a serious deficiency in preparation for the battle of life.

The elder Schopenhauer, who was proud of his business, was bent on seeing his son follow in his steps. For such an aim he believed—and probably prudently—that it would be a mistake to go too far in devotion to general ideas and fundamental principles. Commerce needs not supreme conceptions, but principles of medium range, rules of practical wisdom, derived from the knowledge of the world, and likely to become useless or misleading if refined and rendered too universal. Its knowledge is that of the *media axiomata* —the well-guaranteed maxims of a detailed experience which eschews all scientific idealism. The pure spirit of commerce is cosmopolitan and realist. To its practical estimate history and historical studies are beside the main questions of life; and national interests are counted as mere survivals from an obsolete level of civilization. The study of languages has only an interest because it is a necessity of the commercial situation: an early mastery of the linguistic means of intercourse is indispensable to whoever will win his way in the world. Otherwise the time thus spent is wasted; and Schopenhauer senior might have agreed with Leibnitz that, "if there had been but one language in the world, the human race would have saved a third part of its lifetime which has now to be spent in learning languages."

With views like these young Schopenhauer was to be trained for the merchant career, but so that he should still keep in view the position of a gentleman. Such a combination of characters requires that the pupil should not degenerate into a mere scholar, but keep that graceful mean where culture never goes too far beneath the surface or retires into too reserved and serious profundity. So in 1797, a year after the birth of his only sister Adele, young Arthur Schopenhauer, aged nine, was taken by his father on an excursion to Paris, and then left at Havre in the household of a commercial correspondent, M. Grégoire. There for two years he remained, getting lessons along with the son of the house, young Anthime Grégoire. The two boys soon became fast friends, and in later years often looked back to these happy days of boyhood. In 1799, Arthur went back by sea alone to Hamburg. In the two years' absence he had so thoroughly forgotten his native tongue that his father's heart was delighted. We must remember the time. The elder Schopenhauer belonged in his views to the age before Goethe, and to the Germans of the age of Frederick who had hardly begun to see any traces of the rise of German literature; and who, admirers of Voltaire and his compeers, believed in the superior cosmopolitan value of French and English. At Hamburg Arthur was sent to a private school, frequented by the sons of the wealthier classes, and continued at it for three years. But the boy felt promptings which would not let him rest content with the somewhat "modern" and commercial course which he followed there, and did not control his growing aversion to the career he was destined for. He saw his parents attracted by the society of literary people: his mother in particular setting an especial value on meeting them and having them in her house. Her intellectual tastes found a chord responsive in her son. The ideal of a literary and scholarly life began to fascinate him. He longed to wield the pen, not of the clerk, but of the author. His father, yielding to his persistent entreaties, went so far as to talk of purchasing a canonry for him, to secure his learned ease in the future; but when inquiries on the subject showed that the price of such a benefice would not be small, he abandoned the idea. Then he proceeded to suggest another plan, by which his son was offered the following alternative. On condition of his promising that in the future he would devote himself to a mercantile career, he was to take part in a long excursion to France and England, including a visit to his youthful friend at Havre. If, on the other hand, he stuck to his predilections for the career of learning, he was to remain fixed at Hamburg, prosecuting the study of literature and of Latin. The boy of fifteen could hardly do other than pronounce in favour of the immediate pleasure.

Schopenhauer set out with his parents in the spring of 1803, not to return to Hamburg till New Year, 1805. The travellers (of whose experiences Madame Schopenhauer afterwards published an account) went by Amsterdam and Calais towards England. After spending six weeks in sight-seeing in London, his parents started for a tour in England and Scotland as far as Loch Tay and Inverary, leaving Arthur for the three months they were away in charge of a Rev. Mr. Lancaster at Wimbledon. At this person's boarding-house (he was a clergyman of Merton a few miles off) about sixty boys between the ages of six and sixteen received an ordinary English education, with "music, fencing, and drawing as extras." Two nephews of Lord Nelson (who about this date was living at Merton Place) were among the pupils. Schopenhauer, who also was a "parlour-boarder," found the new manner of life very irksome. The mechanical style of instruction, the long Sunday services, and the regulation march on the Common, were the burden of complaining letters to his mother on his dreary position. She gave a half-serious, half-playful rebuke to his impatient grumbling. He was reminded that he might with advantage put on a more affable and accommodating behaviour, and that a little hard work on literature, especially history, would be better than too ample indulgence in romance and fiction. Above all, he was warned—and many crises in his life show how needful the warning was—that he should put a prompt check on his tendency to bombast and empty pathos. Unfortunately these faults of temper and expression were too radically founded in his nature to be removed, or suppressed, without stern discipline and unfaltering guidance. But his mother's remarks, while they show how the boy was emphatically the father of the man, throw light also on the character of the mother, and on her attitude to her son. They are the words of a somewhat dispassionate observer, whom affection has not blinded to her son's faults, and who does not feel any keen obligation to train firmly and watchfully his errant steps. A little love—or a little severity—would have been a welcome supplement to this purely critical attitude.

Schopenhauer carried away an unfavourable impression of the boarding-school system, and of a good deal of the English character of which it is symptomatic. Like most foreigners, young and old, he was struck by a prevalent tone of cant and hypocrisy, and by the predominance of ecclesiastical interests in ordinary life.

He was beginning to record his impressions of what he saw. But he rarely describes the objective facts; what he notes down are the sentiments they originate in him, the ideas they awaken and define. Not the accumulation of knowledge, but the feeling, the passion, the emotional note it strikes, are what he counts permanently precious. Thus at London, a visit to Westminster Abbey turns his musings to that grand assemblage of great minds in the world beyond the tomb, where the distinctions of time and place and rank that parted them on earth have dropped away, and they meet clad only in the native ornaments of their spirit, in the glory their own might has won. Thus early does he worship genius, and regard power—inborn power and not outward tokens of honour—as the sole thing which can defy the destroying hand of time and death.

In November, 1803, the Schopenhauers left England *viâ* Rotterdam for Paris, after thoroughly inspecting which they proceeded in January, 1804, by way of Tours, Bordeaux, and Nimes to Hyères, and thence back by Lyon and Geneva to Vienna, which was reached about midsummer. Of Arthur's impressions of these scenes all that has been recorded is in illustration of that proclivity his mother accused him of, to " brood over the misery of human beings." On his travels through France, all the charms of the landscape are one day suddenly dispersed by the sight of some wretched huts and the wretched humanity within them —some of those *animaux farouches,—noirs, livides, et tout brûlés du soleil*—at the *tanières où ils vivent de pain noir, d'eau et de racines*, as La Bruyère described them more than a century before. At Toulon he is struck by the hopeless destinies of the galley-convicts; even should they be restored to freedom, the curse of crime clings to them and, in the coldly-averted looks of those around them, drives them back to its weary round. At Lyon he sinks into visions of the gruesome horrors of the Revolution times, as he sees the inhabitants promenading merrily over the square where, some ten years before, their fathers had been massacred by grape-shot. The lad has evidently the uncanny Hamlet-like gift of penetrating beneath the calm and smiling surface of life: he cannot help seeing the skeleton which is grinning horribly in the cupboard. His is a kind of second sight He does not indeed foresee death and doom to come, but in the midst of the banquet of life is haunted by the pallid faces and sightless eyes, which usurp the place of the living. Or (if we borrow by anticipation the metaphor he afterwards took from the East) the "Veil of Mâyâ,"—the illusion, *i.e.*, which envelops the living so that they pass, unseeing, lightly over the crevasses of life, and over its dreary wastes,—is already pierced for him by sudden glimpses of insight into the mystery of the unseen. His was no doubt an abnormal constitution, probably further unstrung by this roving style of life, which facilitated these fits of moody absorption in the inevitable misery of the world. Such a spirit may become a prophet and a seer; it will certainly, by this uncomfortable clairvoyance, not qualify its possessor to play a part in the social comedy or to bear calmly the little worries of existence.

From Vienna he and his parents proceeded to Berlin,

where the father diverged to Hamburg, and left his wife and son to continue their route to Dantzic, where the latter was "confirmed." For about four months, in the office of a Dantzic merchant, Arthur tried to pick up the practice of the counting-house, and did his best, at his father's repeated request, to gain a good business hand in drawing out bills. These injunctions to prepare for the mercantile career are combined in his father's letters with no less insistence on the duty of acquiring a graceful upright carriage, even though he has to get screwed up to the proper posture by accepting a rap across the shoulders for every deviation from the perpendicular.

By the first days of 1805, young Schopenhauer, then close on the completion of his seventeenth year, had taken his place in the office of a senator of Hamburg, named Jenisch. But never, as he himself in self-disparagement admits (in the autobiographical sketch he afterwards wrote for the Berlin faculty), never was there a worse clerk in a merchant's office. Every moment he could he stole from duty to bestow on his favourite authors—a book being ready to be opened as soon as he felt the superintending eye withdrawn. It happened too that in that year Gall, the phrenologist, came to Hamburg to expound his then novel views on mental physiology, which had so gravely shocked Vienna opinion. To attend Gall's lectures on that fascinating topic, the interconnection between mind and body, or rather the direct revelation of spirit in brain, Schopenhauer did not hesitate to adopt the usual subterfuges by which those put under authority seek to cheat their superiors. In such a perverse frame of mind he was abruptly brought to a halt by his father's death. We know little of the latter's mercantile life at Hamburg. But we do know that after the breaking out of war between Germany and the French Republic, the trade of Hamburg had gone rapidly up. The city became the chief *entrepôt* where the colonial produce of Great Britain was exchanged for the corn and timber of the Continent; and the clearing-house for all bills of exchange was the Hamburg Bank. Speculation naturally flourished; fortunes were made and lost with fatal facility; and prices rose enormously. Stocks of goods still went on accumulating, and in 1799 many houses became bankrupt. Latterly these losses seem to have touched Schopenhauer's father. But other things helped. For some years he had been growing deafer; and there had been increasing signs of queerness and irritability. Old friends would be unrecognized and treated as impertinent strangers. At last, in April, 1805, he was found one day precipitated from the upper storey of a granary into the canal, and taken up dead. Whether accident or frenzy caused the calamity remains uncertain; but the balance of suspicion inclines to presume an act of self-destruction.

Upon Arthur the event fell with crushing weight. The father and son had disagreed on the profession to which life should be devoted, but they agreed in many of their estimates of its value. And if young Schopenhauer felt in his heart that he had not been quite loyal to his compact, the feeling would only intensify the bitterness with which his soul was filled. For two years he stuck, though with fearful groans, to his unwelcome post. His mother, at an earlier date, proceeded to make use of her new-gained independence. The business was wound up within a year or so, at some loss, as was to be expected, and the moneys realized were invested in various securities. Johanna, with her daughter Adele (who was ten years old), set off for Weimar, which she reached only a fortnight before the battle of Jena (Oct., 1806). There, at the age of forty, she began a new and freer life. Under the stimulating guidance of Goethe, and the example of the comrades in his Round Table of arts and letters, her slumbering talents found their way to appropriate fields of action, both social and literary. She and her daughter took their part in the round of theatrical performances which formed the staple of life and interest at Weimar. She herself found scope for long-neglected artistic gifts, and learned to use the author's pen. Her house became one of the social centres of Weimar, where Goethe and lesser magnates were often seen. In this development her first adviser and director was K. L. Fernow. Fernow, who is a striking instance how enthusiasm and patience can win for literary ability its appropriate sphere (he had from humble beginnings made himself a distinguished scholar and art-critic), was already stricken by the fatal disease which carried him off in 1808. Between him and the widow a warm friendship sprang up; his critical faculty and knowledge of history helped her over the difficulties of beginning authorship. Her first literary work was to edit the life and memorials of this departed friend; subsequently she attempted, and with considerable popular acceptance, art-biographies, sketches of travel, and works of fiction.

Whilst his mother was thus entering with zest into the light-hearted, generous, but somewhat flimsy Court-Bohemia of letters which gathered round Goethe, Schopenhauer at Hamburg grew more and more dissatisfied with himself, his life, and his surroundings. These broodings in which he indulged take their material from his own feelings and circumstances, but they owe much more to the form which they borrow from the literary predilections of the age. With the later years of the eighteenth century the German world saw the literary movement, which had culminated in the union of Goethe and Schiller, begin to modify its character and pass into the hands of other leaders. The so-called "Romantic School" had begun; in some ways a development of the work begun at Weimar; but in many more a reaction and a protest. Goethe and Schiller had seemed too formal and statuesque, removed by their ideal altitudes and Olympian serenity from the sympathy of the common people, and from the contact of the national life. Truth and light in their purity had been the classical ideal of beauty; a beauty simple, high, and demanding from its worshipper an unselfish love, a severe restraint, a calm enjoyment. Few natures can find entire satisfaction in worship at this formal and ideal shrine. For most there is a craving to mix up art with life, to blend the claims of beauty with the charm of passionate interest. The mere form must receive the colours of emotion, and the dulled sense for pure beauty be stimulated by the attractions of variety, novelty, strangeness. The boundaries of art and science, of art and life, of poetry and religion, had to be broken down, so as to reinforce each by another, and produce a potent elixir of enthusiasm.

To define Romanticism is difficult: its very votaries at this period take it as a watchword, of which they gradually decipher the significance. In antagonism to a period of rationalism, of utilitarianism, and realistic common-sense, of orthodox classical regularity, it upraises the banner of fancy and imagination, of religious and chivalric idealism, of reversion from the commonplace present to the more august past, and calls after it the rare and spiritualized souls who seek a richer and a freer life. It has visions of a human and personal emotion beating at the very centre of all nature and all the process of history, but that not a mere high and philosophic wisdom of love, but a breathing, varying, sympathetic heart, to which every detail of human wish and aim is precious; no general providence, and no moral governor, but an individual heart ready to meet and help in all their fickleness and weakness the human wills that crave for its kindly presence. With such a faith it is inevitable that Romanticism, descending from the altitudes of philosophic idealism and the platform of culture, should seek to get nearer the humble common heart in the ages when man lived, or could be thought to live, nearer to the nature-spirit than now. And so Romanticism turned its back upon science and modern civilization to seek the homes of the natural life, in the medieval world, in the mysterious East, in the so-called superstition of the fireside and the vulgar. Impatient of regularity it grew wild and fantastic, and dwelt by choice in a world where fact is ever leaping up to wed with fancy, however quaint, and which alike for good or ill is the antipodes of this mechanical world in which emotion and sentiment are but powerless interlopers. It had infinite longings and impossible aspirations which nothing finite or temporal can ever satisfy. It delighted in noting what it calls the "irony" of life—the way in which purpose and prudence are in the very instant of accomplishment set at nought by a deeper justice of fate, which unconsciously rules the movement of things. It fancies itself to be recalling a life in grander state and with freer utterance which it lived long ago, and reverts longingly to the heaven it has fallen from. In some cases, where Protestantism seems the very acme of rationalism, Romanticism, strong in religious fervour, will throw itself for shelter and salvation into the bosom of a Catholicism which it imagines as much as finds. But no less may it seek the everlasting hills in the religions of the far-off East, or in pantheistic absorptions. It is weary of that blaze of artificial light which civilization and science and reasoning have spread, and would fain again enjoy the mystery of night, when the heart seems to spread into illimitable space, and can, in the darkness, find a hint and a symptom of presences which make the world less lonely and limited.

At Hamburg Schopenhauer is fully under the sway of such a sentiment, and as his mood is gloomy, his imaginations are perturbed. Life seems to him an intrinsic contradiction—a jest even, though a bitter one. The contrast between its audacious hopes, its yearnings after absolute and entire satisfaction, and its paltry performances, its fruitions spoilt by the sense of deception;

the eternal heavenward aspirations, which, after fluttering feebly round the gates of paradise, sink down to grasp a fulfilment even in dirt and ashes,—the warfare between ideal and real, the restless urgencies, which refuse to be quieted in any sublunary region—these are the recurring tones which dominate his thoughts. In dithyrambic verse he longs to "soar to the throne of the eternal," to "conquer the poor and empty life which can satisfy not one wish out of our infinite longings; to forget the lowly dust on which we have been cast down"; and when emancipated into the life supernal, "in the bodies to see and to love only the spirits." Music alone offered him then, as up to his latest years, some consolations. "The pulses of divine music," he writes, "have not ceased to beat through the centuries of barbarism; and in it a direct echo of the eternal has been left us, intelligible to every capacity and exalted even above virtue and vice."

His mother, perplexed by the lad's despondency and fierce dislike to daybook and ledger, consulted her friend Fernow if it were not too late for her son to begin the preparations for a learned career. Fernow, who had himself passed through a like experience of changed vocation, replied that, with perseverance and talent in the pupil, the age of eighteen was no insuperable barrier to making that acquaintance with the classical languages which forms the preliminary to all higher advances. In fact, as he added, the age of the scholar, if his intellectual powers have been otherwise developed, and if his zeal for knowledge is earnest and steadfast, will only qualify him for acquiring more quickly and rationally the lessons of a classical training. When he received this communication enclosed in a letter which conveyed his mother's assent, Schopenhauer burst into tears of joy, at once sent in his resignation to his principal, and prepared to quit Hamburg. Thus the father's plan for his boy's career was at an end, and the son might seem to have been a defaulter to his faith pledged years ago. And that son himself might then be inclined to accuse his father as a harsh disciplinarian, who had obstinately refused to perceive his peculiar temper and talents. As years passed by, however, he saw more and more how much his father had done for his welfare. He spoke to his young friends of him with gratefulness, told them of the grand house his father had kept, and their grand style of travelling, adding that the merchant is a brilliant exception to the general mean and hypocritical ways of other ranks. But the best evidence of his feelings is to be found in the following passage from his papers; evidently a first draft of a declaration which was meant at one time to stand at the head of the second edition of his chief work :—

"Dedication of the second edition to the *manes* of my father, the merchant, Heinrich Floris Schopenhauer.

"Noble, beneficent spirit! to whom I owe everything that I am. Thy presiding care hath sheltered and borne me, not merely through helpless childhood and unregarding youth, but even in manhood and up to the present day. For, as thou didst bring into the world a son such as I am, thou didst also make provision that in a world like this such a son should be able to subsist and to develop himself. And without this thy care I should have been brought to ruin a hundred times. In my mind the tendency to its only proper vocation was too decidedly implanted to let me do violence to my nature, and so to subjugate it that, recking nought of existence in general, and active only for my personal existence, it should find its sole task in procuring daily bread. Even for this case thou seemest also to have provided, and to have foreseen that he would not be fitted to plough the earth, or by other mechanical industry apply his forces to secure a subsistence; and thou seemest to have foreseen that thy son, thou proud republican, could not possess the talent to compete, *médiocre et rampant*, in cringing before ministers and councillors, Mæcenases and their advisers, basely to beg for the hard-earned piece of bread, or to flatter self-conceited commonplaceness, and humbly join himself to the eulogistic retinue of bungling charlatans; that he, as thy son, would rather think with thy revered Voltaire: *Nous n'avons que deux jours à vivre: il ne vaut pas la peine de les passer à ramper devant des coquins méprisables.*

"Therefore to thee I dedicate my work and hail thee in thy grave with a cry of gratitude, which I owe to thee solely and to no other. *Nam Cæsar nullus nobis haec otia fecit.*

"That I could expand the forces nature gave me, and apply them to their destined purpose, that I could follow my natural instinct and think and work for beings without number, while no one does anything for me: for that I thank thee, my father, thank thy activity, thy prudence, thy thrift and provision for the future. Therefore shall I praise thee, my noble father. And every one who from my work derives aught of joy, consolation, or instruction, shall learn thy name, and know that if Heinrich Floris Schopenhauer had not been the man he was, Arthur Schopenhauer would have been a hundred times ruined. And so let my gratitude do the only thing for thee who hast finished, which I can; let it carry thy name as widely as mine is capable of bearing it."

CHAPTER III.

THE epoch at which Schopenhauer began to seek an entrance through scholarship into the close demesnes of the higher education was a turning-point in philological progress. The old Latin training of the seventeenth century, which set forth as its chief aim the capacity of writing an elegant Latinity, had been considerably discredited by the utilitarian and practical tendencies of the eighteenth. A movement had been vigorously started, under the name of Philanthropinism, to make the methods of teaching more easy and natural, and to give more weight to the bearing of school-lessons on the pursuits of adult life. In extreme forms Philanthropinism probably sank into a vulgar devotion to palpable results, and an undue scorn of more ideal study; but in many ways it was a reasonable protest against a barren service to niceties of grammar, and against a course of classes fitted only to produce schoolmasters. But this divergence from the traditions of a liberal and scholarly instruction led to a corresponding reaction. Classical studies began a new and freer flight. Their champions took the ground that the direct insight into the ideas of the Græco-Roman world, which could only be fully enjoyed by those who were fully masters of the original tongues, was an inestimable instrument in working out that "education into humanity" which was the great desideratum for the higher life in the world of to-day.

A great wave of Greek enthusiasm set in : almost it seemed intoxication. The modern world had disappointed even the most hopeful. Few of those who had, in 1789, greeted the revolt of France against her old monarchy, as if the sun of liberty had at length arisen, still retained, under Napoleon, their generous faith in the Revolution. And the collapse of the old kingdom of Frederick, after 1806, had broken the last hopes of finding salvation in the older state system of Germany. In the darkness and emptiness men turned, as Goethe and Schiller had been leading them, to Greece, to find the inspiration of a freer, more human life. Even a calm philosopher like Herbart propounded a view that classical education should begin with Greek, and that the Odyssey, the tones and colours of which exactly suit the range and temper of the boyish mind, was the right literature on which the boy of from eight to twelve might pasture his adventurous spirit. William von Humboldt, the statesman who helped to mould that educational scheme, under which, with other reforms, began a new era for Prussia, lived and breathed throughout his life the vital air of Greek ideals, moral, religious, and intellectual. And this Hellenic cultus was naturally hostile to the Hebraic elements in religion. Of the new faith the chief hierophant, first at Halle, and afterwards at Berlin, was F. A. Wolf, the prolegomenist to Homer.

He, like his pupil Boeckh, looked forward to a time when Christianity—which in his estimate was only a blending of Greek ethics with Jewish ideas—would be regenerated by being re-absorbed into the purely human ideal of noble life. Like the scholars who first rejoiced in the opening of the literary treasures of Greece at the early Renaissance, they turned from the Bible to the Greeks—only this time it was not to Plato, but to Homer and the poets. The passion for Greece spread everywhere. Hegel, who in 1809 was rector of the Grammar School at Nürnberg, read an address to his boys on the value of the classics for forming a sound heart of national life; and readers of his lectures on the "Philosophy of History" remember the jubilant words with which he leads off the chapter on the Greek world: "With the Greeks we feel ourselves at once at home. . . . Greece presents us the cheerful spectacle of the freshness of youth in the life intellectual." Expressions were sometimes heard of regret that Germany had not derived her lesson of culture directly from Greece, instead of from the more prosaic discipline of Rome.

While hopes ran thus high, Schopenhauer, aged nineteen, was in June, 1807, settled at Gotha, taking his place in the gymnasium or grammar school there beside boys some years junior to him. A position not very wholesome, and likely to create troubles, various according to the temper and capacity of the pupil. He was boarded with one of the masters, and got private lessons from F. W. Doering, a well-known Latinist. But while making prompt advances in his classical studies, he was too wide-awake, and too little inured to regular work, to hide his social lights under a bushel. Soon he became the cynosure of a knot of boys who were captivated by his literary talent and satirical turn, and who egged him on, nothing loath, to display them. A lampoon on one of the masters, whom he barely knew, and about whom he only versified a current scandal, got talked into notice; and, as the authorship of the verses was no secret, Doering, obliged by professional etiquette to resent the insult to his colleague, would have no more to do with his pupil. At his mother's suggestion Schopenhauer next came to Weimar, and there continued his classics under the care of Franz Passow, in whose house he lodged. Passow (whose name figured on the title-page of the early editions of Liddell and Scott's Lexicon) had been called to Weimar as Greek master in 1807, and was only two years older than his pupil. In him we find one of those enthusiasts for all things Greek. It was he who, in a letter written in 1805, precociously said, "The scriptures of the New Testament do much deter me by their horrible Greek." He dreamed, like many of his contemporaries, that the study of Greek literature, and intuition of Greek ideas, would re-awaken in a select few that passion for fatherland and freedom which the bulk of the nation had lost; he claimed for Greek that it should be made the "queen of instruction." It may perhaps be held that Schopenhauer was in too rudimentary a stage to catch the infection of such idealism. But first impressions and first loves leave an indelible trace. He was old enough, and scholar enough, to catch somewhat of that fervour which looked to re-creating the outworn world by a baptismal bath in the ever-living waters of

Greek life and thought; and the spirit which animated Passow at Weimar, and Wolf at Berlin, became a principle moulding his view of life and religion. Without turning into a mere scholar, but taking his part in the lighter occupations of society, making holiday excursions in the neighbourhood, and cultivating his musical tastes, he contrived to make himself a good Greek and Latin scholar. And of that scholarship he was proud—perhaps because it had been won in open and self-imposed effort; and he claimed no less proudly to write for scholars. At a later date he used to regret the disuse of Latin as the language of the republic of letters; spoke with indignant contempt of editions of the Latin authors with German notes: and of an age when German translations (like chicory in place of coffee) drove out the classical originals, would declare that it was a "farewell to humanity, to noble tastes, and high thinking—a return to barbarism, in spite of railways, electric wires, and air balloons." And if his views had prevailed, none would have entered a German University under the age of twenty, and only after passing an *examen rigorosum* in the two ancient languages. So he thought later. But even in the first flush of admiration he worshipped the Greeks. In his copy of Homer there was written (probably later, however) a parody of the Lord's Prayer, addressed to the bard.

But as Schopenhauer advanced in the quest for learning, he drifted farther and farther away from his mother; the diversity of ideas and feelings became more and more palpable. His misadventure at Gotha drew on him sharp rebukes. "You are unbearable and burdensome," she tells him, "and very hard to live with : all your good qualities are overshadowed by your conceit, and made useless to the world, simply because you cannot restrain your propensity to pick holes in other people. So long as you yourself are so open to criticism, people will not put up with your fault-finding, least of all in that offensive oracular style!" She twits him with his vacillations, suspects he is the victim of a bourgeois desire to show off before younger and less privileged friends, and when he removes to Weimar, expresses her fears of violent scenes if they are much together. It is arranged accordingly that he is to stay by himself, but to come daily to her dinner-table from one o'clock to three, and to spend at her house the two evenings weekly on which she is "at home." To know that he is happy is, she declares, necessary to her happiness, but not necessary that she should be a witness to it. And so long as he retains his old character, she will submit to any sacrifices rather than agree to live in the same house with him. His presence, his murmurings over evils irremediable, his gloomy looks, and queer dogmatizing opinions depress her. Her only unpleasant moments are those he causes: and only when he is gone does she breathe freely. If they are to agree, they must consent to live apart.

Such a letter throws its lights on the home life of the Schopenhauers. Madame Schopenhauer is an instance against the theory that marriage and motherhood is the true vocation of every woman; or, at any rate, it proves that there are natures which do not find in their actual wedlock the complementary being through whom their faculties rise into full activity. All along she gives evidence of instincts hankering after a larger sphere, of a sort of spiritual Gypsydom and Bohemianism, to which the restrictions of domesticity are a foolish embarrassment. And now at length she had found a field in which her cravings for independence seemed to find satisfaction. In her superiority of experience and cultivation, she had learned to limit her wants to what the world has to give. Her son, not less bent on self-development than she was, had not yet learned to keep his moods and judgments under control, was uncouth and angular in behaviour, and looked out jealously on those who seemed contented with their quarters. His whole training hitherto had kept him loose from the special ties of life, and not yet having found his way to his due vocation, he wandered as it were restlessly round the gates of society, looking in angrily and uneasily at those who had seized their corner and resolved to keep it. The damsels in the drawing-room would giggle at his grim gaucheries, and even the reproof of a Goethe would hardly convince them that this silent and unapproachable youth could be worth serious attention. If we may trust a portrait made about this time, the future philosopher was a delicate-featured, wistful-eyed, conceited, and reserved young man, with some latent tenderness suggesting itself, but with indications of an exigency that might become hardness. As yet he felt himself engaged with preliminaries only—acquiring the use and mastery of his tools, and taking in the perspective of the situation—oppressed and out of sorts occasionally with the drudgery inevitable at such a stage.

But there were special circumstances which strained the bond of kindred till it broke. His mother was by no means a Clytæmnestra, or like Hamlet's guilty mother. But there is something analogous in the position of the son who, coming home after a temporary exile, finds his father already forgotten, and his mother on terms of intimate friendship with first one and then another of the literary knights-errant of Weimar. His own intense and exacting mood, with the feeling of spiritual kindred to the departed, makes his blood boil within him to see his mother, still conscious of no lack of charms, gaily entering into full possession of herself, drinking in gladly the admiration of young and old who find themselves drawn by the fresh sympathy and wealth of natural womanliness in this new accession to the ranks of the *émancipées*. In such a temper, when the heart as it were reels at the sight of the fickleness of affection and the abyss of disloyalty, Schopenhauer fell back on solitary meditations on the radical selfishness and pettiness of life. Thus we find him at Weimar, in 1808, writing, " If we take out of life its few moments of religion, of art, and of pure love, what is left but a long series of trivial thoughts ? " And at a later date he moralizes : " The pain we pass on from ourselves to another is only augmented thereby : hence the mass of ills in the world caused by egotistically pushing onwards the primary evil. It is only by voluntarily taking on ourselves this ill in its first positive shape that it can be most effectively, perhaps utterly, diminished, and then the kingdom of God will come." With these mournful soliloquizings there not unnaturally went signs of physical disturbance. Fierce fits of panic and despair would sweep over him, especially in the night season: fears and unaccountable suspicions would torment him, as they occasionally did in later life: and his nerves would be shaken beyond all self-control by tragic scenes. But if he was abnormally sensible to the misery prowling behind the surface of life, his pessimism had a not distant consolation in his philosophy. The essence of philosophy was for him the assurance that "there is a spirit world, where, separate from all the appearances of the outer world, we can, in detachment and absolute repose, survey them from an exalted seat, however much our bodily part may be tossed in their storm." It is, in other words, the "assurance that outside man there is something which knows and feels him as he feels himself." A time came when that consolation had to take another phase: when atheism will seem a more proper name for his philosophy than theism. For, as he then wrote (1844): "With the world alone has philosophy to do, and it leaves the gods at rest: expecting however in return that it will be left at rest by them." Yet perhaps the change of creed was not so deep in reality as it sounds in formula.

In the beginning of 1809 Schopenhauer, on attaining his majority, received his share of the paternal fortune, amounting to about 19,000 thalers. Some 6,000 of this sum lay on loan at Dantzic, bearing at first 8 and latterly 6 per cent. interest: the rest was invested in real securities. Besides this, he had his part-interest in the properties at Ohra and elsewhere in the vicinity of Dantzic: which, let out to tenants, were valued in 1799 at 40,000 gulden, but for some years yielded little rent. In all, Schopenhauer about this date had a yearly income of 1,000 thalers (about £150), and the sum was afterwards increased by legacies, *e.g.*, on the death of his uncle Andreas in 1816. Thus, being now considered ripe for college, and provided with what, for the time and country, was a very fair stock of world's goods (very different from the scanty equipments of Kant or Fichte), he entered himself in October, 1809, at the University of Göttingen. University study was still considered as a means of preparation for one of the learned professions, and a student was expected to label himself at starting with the faculty he ultimately meant to practise. The pursuit of a study for its own native attractions, was not encouraged and even barely permitted. Schopenhauer enrolled his name as a student of medicine: a choice indicating at the least a predilection for the science of the physical microcosm; and for the first year the lectures he heard were chiefly on physical science. In his second winter, however, he turned to philosophy.

The year 1810, in which he thus found his calling, marked a low-water level in the philosophic tide. The influence of Kant's ideas through Germany had begun to be felt first of all at Jena, which was the home of the new philosophy as Weimar was of the new poetry. At Jena, indeed, for a while poetry and philosophy walked hand in hand. What Reinhold had initiated in 1786— a reconstitution of Kantism by a regress to deeper principles—had been carried on, from 1794 onwards, with rapid steps and dazzling variety by Fichte, Schiller, and Schelling, as well as by others now less known to fame.

To the years from 1794 to 1799 Fichte's principal systematic works belong; while the years after 1799 are the most productive period of Schelling. But since the catastrophe of 1806 a lull had set in. The fall of Prussia led to the temporary closing of the University of Halle, and the most distinguished teachers began to look for posts in Bavaria and elsewhere. But with the year 1810 hopes of better things began. In that year the new University was founded at Berlin (where numerous informal courses of lectures had been given for the twenty years preceding), and Fichte re-entered the academic lecture-room. Göttingen meanwhile, like Halle, had been among the places which still clung to the old half-sceptical, half-formal, common-sense philosophy which Meiners and Feder had taught, and which they tried to defend against this new invasion of what they deemed Berkeleyan idealism.

The teacher through whom Schopenhauer was initiated into the formal mysteries of what he afterwards held to be his vocation, was G. E. Schulze. He was a new professor, called to Göttingen in 1810 from the (now extinct) university of Helmstädt (between Brunswick and Magdeburg), and probably there was a curiosity to hear the author of "Aenesidemus" (published 1792), the work on which rests the now somewhat shadowy reputation of Schulze in the history of philosophy. That work was an event in the war of pamphlets which raged between the followers of Kant and the upholders of other modes of thought. It was an attempt to prove that the "Critical" philosophy—the professed enemy of dogmatism—was itself highly dogmatic, to show that while professing to be a philosophy of experience, and to confine all sound knowledge to the task of exploring the natural world, it had yet allowed the unknowable supernatural, the "thing-in-itself," to exert a very real influence on consciousness. But it was not this book which led to Schopenhauer's conversion to philosophy, but rather the advice of Schulze to his pupil at first to confine himself to reading Plato and Kant, and, till he had mastered them, to leave Aristotle, Spinoza, and the rest alone. Followed the advice certainly was. If we merely consult the words of his philosophy, we might say it turns entirely upon "Plato the divine and the marvellous Kant," as he has styled them. But he approached the study of them, *parti pris*, with an idea, a single idea, already forming in his mind. And hence he came to find them only presenting the complementary aspects of truth, of which his own philosophy is to reveal the essential identity. Though a professed follower of Kant, he constantly marks his divergence, and shows a more dominating interest in the supernatural. He uses the forms of Kantian thought to give a historical position and aspect to his ideas of the contrast between appearance and reality. And in Plato he sees exclusively the mystical and ascetic philosopher who banished true reality to a transcendent world, the very antithesis of the changeable scenes of temporal and corporeal existence. Kant and Plato, in short, serve simply to clear up his own mind; they afford the pegs on which he hangs his thought, the machinery and terminology through which his system is woven into definite outline. Of the historical position, and of the psychological development, of the two writers themselves, he has no care. And this procedure stamps his work throughout. Even after his main idea—his theory of life and being—was formulated and published, he sits still, waiting like the spider on his web, ready to snap up every bit of scientific experience and every scrap of literature for the further elaboration and illustration of his theme. Every piece of knowledge is at once evaluated as a possible confirmation. His is a philosophy which, instead of extending in wide periphery, drags everything down to its centre.

As on a former occasion, the vigorous prosecution of study was never carried by Schopenhauer to an extent inconsistent, either with the care of health, or the culture of social amenities. This at least was one lesson which his father's mercantile drill had impressed on him, that the professional study should never make him lose sight of the ideals of a gentleman. He cultivated his musical talents, in which he had found so much charm and consolation. He had mastered the flute; now he made imperfect acquaintance with the guitar. With several of his fellow-students he was on friendly terms, especially Bunsen, subsequently the friend of princes and scholars, and a German-American, Astor, the second in the well-known line of millionaires. Bunsen, who was then in poor circumstances, received from him substantial evidence of friendship; nor was he the only acquaintance with whom Schopenhauer communicated some of his more than average means. In society he was notorious for his determination always to keep to the front, and to have his views endorsed by general acceptance, and many a wager sealed to his cost his belief in his own infallibility. In the holidays he would go on short tours, *e.g.*, to the Harz mountains. On the occasion of a visit to Weimar, he paid a call on Wieland, then seventy-eight years old. The poet spoke to him of the choice of a vocation, and dissuaded him from the life of a philosopher. The young man replied, "Life is an awkward business (*missliche Sache*); I have determined to spend it in reflecting on it." Perhaps the meeting was not altogether fortuitous. But if his friends supposed the veteran man of letters might divert him from the adventurous path of free thought, or even of literary and academic success, they were doomed to disappointment. Wieland at the close of their interview could but wish him well in his chosen career.

At the end of the summer of 1811, Schopenhauer changed his quarters to the University of Berlin, then in its second year of existence. Here, as before, his chief attention was bestowed upon the natural sciences, to all those inquiries, such as physics, chemistry, botany, anatomy, &c., which lead up to physiology, "the summit of the whole of natural science," he would term it, "and its obscurest region." "Psychology," he would add, "is nothing; for there is no psyché or soul; you cannot study man for himself alone, but only in connection with the world, macrocosm and microcosm at the same time." A drastic expression, indeed, but entirely valid against the merely introspective method, which fancies it can gain truth by an abstractly inward observation, and analyses human understanding as it would a plant. He further attended lectures on the History of Philosophy by Schleiermacher, and on Greek Literature and Antiquities by Wolf. In the year 1811-12 he heard Fichte lecture on "Facts of Consciousness" and "Theory of Science," and, in the conversational or dialogue lectures which the professor gave, Schopenhauer, according to his own belief, shone as a disputant. Apparently he also took copies from the notes of lectures which he did not personally attend.

That he did not waste his college days is proved by the ponderous note-books which he left behind with the fruits of his attendance in the class-room. But these same documents evidence that the young gentleman already considered himself a better philosopher than any of his teachers, and that the contempt he so abundantly lavished on the "university-professor" in later years was a prejudice of old standing in his constitution. In these notes Schulze is at one place styled a "cattle-beast," and at another a "sophist"; his doctrines are summarily dismissed as "nonsense," or "twaddle." A remark of Schleiermacher, that "No man can be a philosopher without being religious," is put aside with the emendation that "No man who is religious takes to philosophy; he does not need it. Nobody who really philosophizes is religious; he walks without leading-strings, dangerous but free." But the vials of the young critic's self-conceit are poured most liberally, and with efforts to be facetious, on Fichte. The professor had gone beyond his hearer's depth (for in those days his utterances were laboured and involved, unlike his old rush of words): "In this hour," notes the listener, "besides what is here written down, he said things which made me wish I could put a pistol to his breast, saying, Die thou must without remedy; but for thy poor soul's sake tell whether, in uttering such stuff, thou hadst any distinct idea, or didst merely befool us." And, at another time, as the lecturer expounded how each existence is constituted by its relation to another, the note is appended: "In these days in the dark (when the tallow-candles did not enter into visibility) he said quite beautiful things of an Other."

Petulancies like these would be beneath recording were they not so characteristic of the life-long attitude of the man to antagonistic modes of thought, and did they not derive some importance from the charges of plagiarism from Fichte and Schleiermacher that have been brought against him. To trace resemblances between the characteristic ideas of a philosopher and anticipations or adumbrations of them in earlier thinkers is always a somewhat invidious and fantastic task. And if one is to track back all modern notions to the audacious mortals who said them before, little originality would be left. Up to a certain point every philosopher is an eclectic; he creates not new ideas, but new formulæ; he finds and polishes old pearls of thought, and sets them as new systems. Moreover, if even the most opposing systems of an epoch are yet complementary to each other, they rest on common foundations, and are deeply modified by the theories they controvert. It is not strange, therefore, to find in Schopenhauer a good deal that sounds like the assonance of what Fichte and Schleiermacher had taught. And, in general, it is incontrovertible that his work has occasionally the aspects of an ill-adjusted mosaic; the parts have got a common tone, but they are not inwardly harmonized to the requisite systematic unity ; their principle of synthesis is subjective and personal, rather than objective and intrinsic. These similarities between his ideas and those of preceding writers are sometimes not less than in the case of Fichte. Thus, as has been recently pointed out, his doctrine that the world is no mere idea, but also a Will, had been partly anticipated in the work of a Göttingen Professor, Bouterwek, whose "Idea of an Apodictic" was published in 1799. And yet it is highly improbable that he had studied this work. Unconscious similarities are far from rare, just as they are far from inexplicable.

In the case of Fichte, that intense personality which made his colleagues at Berlin accuse him of a conviction that he, and he alone, was the chosen vehicle of the spirit of reason, would naturally not commend him to an obstinate and ambitious mind like Schopenhauer. The latter already felt he had a system within him, and could not brook a rival authority, especially one not less domineeringly dogmatic than himself. Especially, too, when a resemblance in fundamental metaphysical ideas, not imperceptible to careful eyes, was interpreted and distorted by the immense difference of practical moral tone—Fichte, in the bright triumphant flight of his idealism, supported by faith in a moral order of the world which works for righteousness, turning his back on "the darker ethics of self-torture and mortification," and rushing into the political and social fray, proclaiming the duties of patriotism, idealizing the soldier, calling to and exercising an active philanthropy, living with his nation, and continually urging it upwards to higher levels of self-realization—Schopenhauer, recurring to the ideals of asceticism, preaching the blessedness of the quiescence of all will, disparaging efforts to save the nation or elevate the mass, and holding that each has enough to do in raising his own self from its dull engrossment in lower things to an absorption in that pure passionless being which lies far beyond all, even the so-called highest, pursuits of practical life.

The difference between the two men came out in 1813. Schopenhauer up to that time had been busiest apparently in gaining a fuller experience of physical and physiological fact. He had gone often to the hospital, La Charité, to study cases of mental and bodily disease; interested, like the "Realist" and "Naturalist" he was, in the pathology of human nature, the dark places where it is less careful to keep its secret. During these years a gloom had settled on Prussia, reduced to half its extent by the peace of Tilsit, and its capital, like its chief fortresses, held by a French garrison. At length came the disaster of Napoleon in Russia, and, following it, the summons to the nation to rise against the invader. The classes were broken up before the close of the session, and students and professors began to drill in the *Landsturm*. Fichte with his wife stayed on to work, to help in the care of the wounded, and finally, next January, to die at his post. Schopenhauer was an alien in the land; and perhaps did not forget that the robbed in 1813 had been the robbers of Poland in 1793. Perhaps, like Goethe, he felt inclined to tell the Germans to "shake away at their chains; the man was too great for them." Yet not altogether unmoved by the excitement around, he contributed towards equipping volunteers for the army. Physical cowardice and want of sympathy with the movement kept him back from active service. What was Germany to him? A mere geographical unity, created by historical accidents, and preserved by national prejudice. After the battle of Lützen (fought May 2nd), when Berlin seemed endangered, and some of its inhabitants fled to Silesia for safety, Schopenhauer set out to seek a shelter at Dresden. When he got there, after a journey of twelve days, in which the chances of war had obliged him to play the part of interpreter between a French officer and the people of a Saxon town, he judged it wise to hurry on to Weimar. Even there he did not stay; his mother's domestic arrangements were by no means to his mind, and from June to November, 1813, he took up his quarters in an upper chamber of the inn *Zum Ritter* at Rudolstadt, a principality to the south of Weimar, employing his leisure in the composition of an essay. Originally meant as an exercise to qualify for the degree of Doctor of Philosophy at Berlin, it was now offered to the University of Jena with the same intent. The diploma was granted on the 2nd of October, and before the end of the year the work appeared from the press at Rudolstadt as "Philosophical Treatise on the Fourfold Root of the Principle of Sufficient Reason." The book, published at his own cost, was a thin octavo of 148 pages. In after-days it was promoted by its author to the rank of first part of his system, and described as a preliminary treatise which his readers must have mastered if they wish really to understand him. And, in accordance with this view, the second edition, which appeared in

1847, was subjected to extensive alterations in the way both of omission and addition, so as to correspond more exactly with the teaching of his later treatises. The original edition, which is now rare, seems to have excited no general notice. Its title gave his mother subject for a joke, that it savoured somewhat of the herbalist's shop; and when he retorted that his book would be read when a copy of her works would scarcely be found even in a lumber-room, she could reply that at that time the whole edition of his would still be procurable.

Schopenhauer's essay discusses a topic which is as old as philosophy itself, and one which, under the disguise of a problem in abstract logical analysis, has important metaphysical bearings. But in its original structure and finish it bears witness to the circumstances of its origin. Its author has not yet acquired that facility of style, especially of illustration, which distinguishes his later work; he has not yet arrived at that self-contained sense of his own independence or originality which he afterwards assumes. It is an essay written for the purpose of displaying his ability as a philosophical analyst, and with a view to the judgment of an academic board. It is a *ballon d'essai* and an *œuvre d'occasion:* not the outpouring of his whole mind and soul. It is written, too, under the full influence of his apprehension of Kant's idealism—with parade of the distinction and correlation of subject and object. Yet, even under these conditions, his characteristic views do not fail to emerge.

The quaint title of the book—and his titles have always a smack of paradox—refers to the four phases which the process of assigning a reason for, or explaining, a thing severally assumes, as it belongs to one or other of the four branches of knowledge,—physical science, mathematics, logic, and ethics. The common rubric—cause or reason—is traced back to four very distinct roots, the contrasts between which are expounded briefly but suggestively. In a way perhaps most of the work had been done before—partly by Kant in his earlier essays—but never perhaps had it been done so simply and decisively. Undoubtedly there is danger of confusing, as of exaggerating these distinctions. A thinker like Spinoza treats the "cause" and the "because" as identical, and applies a mathematical method of argument to philosophy. Many a writer on the question of Free-will has reduced motivation to a mere case or instance of general physical causation; and it has been again and again assumed that reasoning from major and minor premiss to conclusion is the type to which, *e.g.*, even mathematical reasoning must conform.

Now, to take the last point first—as it was the part of the book which first found, and naturally, a response in the mind of Goethe—Schopenhauer directs his weapons against the habit unduly to magnify the power of reasoning,—by which he means abstraction and generalization. The mere reasoner deals with truth only at second hand; originally truth is given by perception—by the intuition of experience. Science has its firm and fertile basis in intelligent observation; reasoning only supervenes to formulate in general terms the discoveries of individual genius. Thus, the man who really makes science advance must be a seer. And this is especially true of mathematics. The form in which Euclid has thrown his propositions disguises, according to Schopenhauer, the real movement, which is a gradually intensified perception of the relation of elements in a geometrical figure. The formal proof is only an outward scaffolding, which, while it helps so far, finally must be supposed removed, so that the eye may really take in the full meaning of the building. It only helps the mind to see, and has no value of its own. Yet so insidious is the habit of logical demonstration that its devotees would like to prove everything—even the axioms or common notions on which mathematics reposes. But, in a further degree, this tendency leads to the confusion between logical consecution and real sequence; between the order of subordination or inference in thought, and the connection of causality between things. Schopenhauer, insisting that the real nerve of science is in intelligent judgment, and not in reasoning, carries almost *ad absurdum* that antithesis between sense-limited intellect and supra-sensible reason which Kant had made current in speculation.

Hardly less characteristic is his view of the relations between physical and moral causation. Imperfectly worked out in the first edition, it yet leads up to the doctrine that motivation is causation seen from the inside. Usually, by our own empiricist writers, for instance, causality is employed to throw light—or rather darkness—on the question of motivation. Causality they in general treat as an accidental idea, deposited *at length* as a sediment from accumulated experiences. Schopenhauer, who had absorbed the *à priori* from Kant till it dominate his whole philosophy, briefly starts from the position that causality is the very essence and function of all intellect alike in animals and in man. But as applied in the physical world,—its proper domain,—causality merely means that every phenomenon is really the prolongation or continuation of another preceding it, and to know the law of causality is to possess the formula for calculating the later from the earlier. Into the inner meaning of this sequence we do not penetrate, but are mere external observers of the fact. But in motivation "we stand as it were behind the curtain, and learn the secret how the cause in its innermost nature induces the effect;" we are, in other words, supposed to be directly aware of the inner bond of union between cause and effect. For, whereas, in physical causation, the cause and effect are both "objects" to me, the "subject" (subject and object being thus different and apart), in the case of the will or motivation I am both subject and object—subject of knowledge in so far as I know, object of knowledge in so far as I will to act. This identity between the "I who know" and the "I who will" is the great and perpetual miracle of mental life; the "phenomenon *par excellence*," which distinguishes us from the world of which we only see the outside. And in this fact lies the key to the explanation of natural causation; if nature too be a will, which, however, has not yet attained to consciousness and cognition of itself, not yet become an Ego. But the further discussion of this view belongs to the account of Schopenhauer's chief book.

The war, meanwhile, had been raging, and troops,

French, Russian, Austrian, and Prussian, were marching and countermarching from town to town in Germany. But Rudolstadt lay out of the line of retreat and pursuit, and in his inn the philosopher enjoyed tolerable tranquillity. At length, when his first book had been launched on the world, the author, now aged twenty-five, returned in November, 1813, to Weimar. Forgetful of past disagreements, he for a few months boarded with his mother. It need hardly be said that the experiment turned out a disastrous failure. If he could not get on with her while he was still under wardship, harmony was less likely now that he had lived by himself for four years. Tendencies to friction were sure to be multiplied where an artificial relation supplanted, without annihilating, the natural bond of parentage. The son, suspicious by nature, thought his mother was reckless of the future; and the mother, light-hearted and sociable, resented the interferences of her exacting son. He had introduced a poor student friend of his own into the house, and maintained him there for a couple of months. This intrusion his mother did not relish. There was already domiciled with her — for accommodation was scanty in Weimar — a man nearly nine years older than her son, Friedrich von Müller. Von Müller, who had come to the town only a few years before, was already a trusted public servant of the Grand Duke; he is the Chancellor von Müller, whose reminiscences and characteristics of Goethe have been translated into English by Sarah Austin. To this courtier young Schopenhauer took a violent aversion, and behaved with such outrageous rudeness that Von Müller, in a moment of passion, broke out fiercely on him. All this was supremely disturbing to the lady. At first she suggested that her son should take other quarters for himself, on the ostensible ground that she was losing money by the boarding arrangement. But he was not the man to take a hint and go. He asked to have the price raised to a suitable amount. To this proposal his mother returned—as she had for some time done, after finding verbal communications disagreeable—a written reply. She pointed out that in her opinion it was inconvenient and undesirable for a grown-up son to occupy the same house with his mother. He was, she found, too dogmatic, too contemptuous of those unlike him, too needlessly peremptory in manner, and too much inclined to preach at her. She could not, she thought, be expected, for the sake of a son with whom it was clear that she could never hope to get on, to dismiss a friend who was faithful and helpful to her, and who made her life pleasanter, merely because that friend was unacceptable to her son. One of them evidently had to go, and she had already stated her views unmistakably on her son's incompatibility. Accordingly, in May, 1814, he quitted his mother and Weimar. His mother, who lived for twenty-four years longer, he never saw again, though correspondence was resumed between them about six years before her death.

It is easy to say, and there is a cheap truth in the statement, that there were faults on both sides. It is perhaps equally cheap moralizing to say that his want of filial piety is shocking. Perhaps we may, as often happens, find in his *Parerga und Paralipomena* a generalized statement of his own special case. "All women," he there declares, "are, with rare exceptions, inclined to extravagance. Any existing property, therefore, with exception of the rare cases where they have themselves acquired it, should be secured against their folly. I am therefore of opinion that women should never be quite allowed to manage their own concerns, but always stand under actual male supervision, be it of father, of husband, of son, or of the state—as is the case in Hindostan; and that consequently they should never be given full power to dispose of any property they have not themselves acquired. The contrary practice, to wit, that a woman can actually become the appointed guardian and administratrix of the paternal inheritance of her children, I hold to be a piece of unpardonable and pernicious folly. In the majority of instances, such a woman will take what the children's father acquired through the labour of his whole life, and acquired through the stimulus of his care for them, and will spend it with her paramour, whether she marries him or not." And he goes on to quote Odyssey xv. 20, where the owl-eyed Athene warns Telemachus of the risks his patrimony runs from Penelope's suitors. And to the same effect in the paragraphs "On Women" in the same work: "Women should never have free disposition over heritable property, *i.e.*, funds, houses, and landed estates. They constantly require a guardian (tutor), and accordingly should in no possible case be made the guardians of their children. The vanity of women, even though not greater than that of men, has the misfortune to be directed wholly on material things, viz., first on their personal beauty, and secondly on gaudy show and splendour. Hence 'society' is properly their element: and this makes them, especially considering their slight reasoning powers, inclined to extravagant expenditure." Whatever truth there may be in these disclosures of feminine weaknesses, the tone and circumstances of their utterance betray a sordid nature. The chief merit for which he hymns his father's praises had been his prudent accumulation of wealth to facilitate the son's future life of study, and now the main gravamen of his censure on his mother is her pecuniary negligence, endangering his chances of independence.

Long years after, one of his youthful admirers, to whom he had expressed the repugnance he felt to the circles at Weimar in which his mother lived, sent Schopenhauer a copy of a passage from Anselm von Feuerbach's Memoirs (published in 1852), in which he speaks of his acquaintances at Karlsbad in 1815. It gives the outspoken criminalist's opinion of the Schopenhauer family. " Madame Schopenhauer, a rich widow. Makes profession of erudition. Authoress. Prattles much and well, intelligently; without heart and soul. Self-complacent, eager after approbation, and constantly smiling to herself. God preserve us from women whose mind has shot up into mere intellect." Schopenhauer, thanking his correspondent for the extract, finds the description true to nature, and adds that he "could not, God forgive him, keep from laughing."

We must pass from the painful subject and say no

more of one of those domestic feuds where bitterness inexplicable interposes between near kinsfolk. But, on the other hand, we need not exaggerate the dimensions of a family squabble, or accept every word of bombast. Something may be allowed here to the idiosyncrasy of the son which makes him his own accuser—that fierce petulance of words in which he loses himself and wounds blindly.

It is often said that great men owe to their mothers much of their character and talent. But Schopenhauer, with an attempt at greater precision, maintained that the will was inherited from the father, the intellect from the mother; and he probably held the personal belief that his own case showed a vigorous development of both, and a no less vigorous antithesis between them. The generalization is an instance of his habit of using his own case as a rule of explanation, and of his failure to get beyond popular distinctions to their real foundation. What is Will, and what is Intellect, he nowhere adequately explains; he simply repeats, as a thing self-evident, the contrast of terms. But if anything may be said to be certain in psychology, it is the impossibility of severing will from intellect by any inflexible line. The scientific analysis of what underlies the popular distinction has yet to be made. And not merely have notable thinkers refused to accept the absolute disjunction; language in its oldest and most natural forms equally ignores this thorough-going disjunction of heart from head, feeling from thought. A subtler chemistry than this mechanical union is moreover at work in the mental organization, and to speak of the *laws* of intellectual and moral heredity is as yet decidedly premature. The general fact known as heredity is palpable: its conditions most indefinable.

But at Weimar there had been compensating interests for him—business in higher regions than the ignoble sphere of family conflicts. The great Goethe, struck by the appreciation of intuition and realism in his dissertation, fancied he had found an ally in the battle he had been waging against the abstract conceptions of the scientific physicists. Since 1791-2, when he published his "Optical contributions," Goethe had held to his conviction that the Newtonian theory of Light was a mistake. But the result of his reflections and observations, which he brought out in 1810 as a "colour-theory" (Farbenlehre), had been received by the scientific public with a contemptuous silence for which he was unprepared. According to Goethe, the true achievement of science is to get at the real fact—to see the actual concrete problem stripped of all excrescences and accidents—not, as the ordinary scientist believes, to find an explanation at all hazards for a fact which he has never really *ascertained*, really fixed in its primal phenomenon. The optical philosopher, therefore, instead of forming hypotheses about the nature of light, has to give the complete history of its effects. "Colours are the acts of light—its activities and passivities. In that sense we can expect from them information about light." But they must be studied in connection with nature as a whole: "for it is nature as a whole which thus reveals itself to the sense of the eye." And the observer is not a mere onlooker; his glance must be attentive; he must, in short, theorize. "'To do so consciously, with self-knowledge, with freedom,—to employ a bold word—with irony, such skill in observation is necessary if the abstractness we fear is to be harmless, and the experiential result we look for is to be truly fresh and useful." But such a theory differs from what is so called by scientists, because, in Goethe's judgment, it has *seen* the fact in its totality and in reference to the whole complex of nature. He thus comes to the conclusion that the colours are results due to the comparative translucency or opaqueness of the medium through which the original agents of nature, light and darkness, present themselves to the eye. Goethe takes, *e.g.*, a Bohemian drinking glass—such as he sent in 1821 to Hegel, another of his partisans in this fray—and, covering its inside margin, one half with black, the other half with white, shows that these portions respectively appear as blue and yellow. Such an experiment presents an *Ur-phänomen* of colour.

In hope of securing for his intuitions and theories a friend who would be better able to take the poetico-speculative standpoint than the ordinary man of science, Goethe sent Schopenhauer some of his optical appliances, showed him a few of the more unusual and striking experiments, and waited for the support he felt sure of. "Dr. Schopenhauer," writes Goethe in his "Annalen," "stepped to my side as a friend and well-wisher. We dealt with many things in mutual agreement, yet at last a certain division became inevitable, as when two friends who have hitherto gone together say good-bye—the one, however, wanting to go north, the other south, so that they very quickly lose sight of each other." Schopenhauer accepted the view as an adequate description of the physical colours, those, *i.e.*, produced by material means, in themselves colourless, and only permitting light to more or less pass through them. But the old antagonism between the poet, with his ingrained aversion to the introspective method and his disposition to build on the sure apprehension of external reality, and the philosopher, always harking back from the visible to the invisible, and inclined to raise each question to its most abstract or generalized phase, soon showed itself. The problem itself, as well as others which lay nearer his own heart, Schopenhauer carried with him to Dresden, whither he retired towards the end of May, 1814, and where for the ensuing four years he was a permanent resident. By the autumn of next year he sent to Goethe a manuscript containing his conclusions on the matter, and a slight correspondence between the two ensued in the winter. The essay was published at Easter, 1816, under the title *Ueber das Sehen und die Farben* ("On Vision and Colours"). In 1830 a somewhat abbreviated and modified Latin version of the essay, written by Schopenhauer himself, was inserted in a collection of *Scriptores Ophthalmologici Minores*, edited by Justus Radius.

The essay, which takes up what its author calls a physiological or subjective attitude, assumes that colours are in the eye, and only in the eye, while light is, somewhat inconsistently, treated as an external agent, supplying the primary stimulus to which colours are the response of the eye. So far he starts from the natural realism of Goethe. The first chapter of the essay expounds his view of the distinction between sensation and perception. In the first weeks of the child's life we have no reason to suppose that there is more than a peculiar feeling in the retina, comparable to the crude splash of paints on an artist's palette. When intelligence awakes, this *sensation* is abruptly and at one swoop translated into the *perception* of a coloured object. This intelligence is the characteristic endowment of the animal world, and is essentially an act of causal reference —an act which instantaneously and unconsciously interprets these sensations on the retina into the effects produced by an object.—The theory may be left without criticism, until one can obtain an authorized explanation of phrases like "modification of the senses," or "affection of the eye."

The rest of the monograph deals with the theory of Colours. The modern physiological optics find the phenomena of colour-perception to depend on certain varieties of structure in the terminals of the nerves of vision ; a certain triplicity in the anatomy of the retina. Schopenhauer's theory has been styled an aperçu, of which the other is an empirical justification and correction. He treats colours as due to a "qualitative division" in the activity of the retina in response to light. What that "qualitative division" is, otherwise than as it expresses itself in colour, he cannot tell us. All he can say is that the eye is so constituted that, in response to certain stimuli of light, it breaks up that response into two parts—parts, however, which are of unlike quality. Yet, unlike as they are in quality, these two parts are so related to each other that they are mutually complementary. Colour, in short, is an optical polarity—a tendency to split up into dissimilar parts—which dissimilar parts yet bear a ratio to each other in constituting the whole—*i.e.*, light. In form, this tendency is illimitable; there may be an endless variety of pairs of shades and colours; but in pairs the colours will always go. Some of them, however, stand out among the rest, distinguished by the simple fractions (with denominators 2, 3, or 4) which represent the ratio of the two polarly-opposed parts. These are the more primary and fundamental colours. When the balance is even, and each part is exactly half of the total activity, we get the complementary colours, red and green, the harmonious centres of the scale of colour; then come orange and blue, which are to each other as 2 to 1; and thirdly, yellow and violet, which form respectively ¾ and ¼ of the total. Each colour, therefore, is equally uncompounded; the only difference is that other shades than those named represent a less simply-perceived ratio between complementary parts.

Such a new theory of colour need not detain us long. As a hypothesis, it is ingenious and fantastic. The numerical proportions which Schopenhauer assigns cannot be verified by any experimental evidence; they rest, as he naïvely admits, on an "intuitive" certainty, and are detected merely by feeling; they are, in short, a picturesque and sham-precise way of stating that an æsthetic relation (such as that formulated by the "golden section") may be surmised to underlie the harmonies and contrasts of colour. But, so far as experimental authority and consequent accuracy go, they are not less fatally deficient than the numerical proportions which Plato has assigned to the combination of the elements. Schopenhauer was wont to boast of his scientific studies, in which, as he imagined, he had set an example of honest preparation which his ambitious contemporaries would have done well to imitate. Yet, after all, it may be doubted whether, in the absence of a mathematical grounding, he had got more acquaintance with the materials of science than was capable of helping him to body out, with more detail and show of scientific imagination, hypotheses which still remain fantastic and vague. Like the "Natur-philosophie" in general, under which his essay falls as a specimen, his force lies, not in the ascertainment of physical elements or conditions in the structure and functions of the organ of sense, which would account for the phenomena of coloured vision, but in the attempt to describe, or formulate, the essence of the fact under more general categories or potencies.

CHAPTER IV.

OF the four years (1814–1818) during which Schopenhauer made his home at Dresden, there is little in the way of event to record. His dwelling was a quiet house in the Ostra-Allee, not far from the Zwinger and its picture-gallery. He had of course acquaintances among the second-rate literary and artistic notabilities of the place. J. G. von Quandt, an art-critic, perhaps deserves special mention; but friends probably were rare. His manner did not attract: in his earnestness and self-absorption he was apt to grow emphatic, to press on regardless of personal feelings, and thus got an ill-repute for a loud and dictatorial style, and the nickname of *Jupiter tonans*. Doubtless he was an occasional visitor to the art-collections of the place; but not as a student of their history and archæology, rather to learn the revelation they might have to give of the meaning of life and the worth of things. To the theatre and the concert-room he probably went about as regularly as he afterwards did. And there were other attractions. But of this there is no history. What interest his biography has is an inward interest, and even that is slight; for it turns again and again on the same ideas and the same struggles.

Already at Weimar—and probably earlier—he had been pondering over the antagonism in human nature—the dissatisfaction which springs eternal in the human breast as we contrast each relative fulfilment with the infinite possibility. "Inward discord," he writes at Dresden in his note-books of 1814, "is the very law of human nature, so long as a man lives. He can be only one thing actually and thoroughly; and yet for everything else he has a potentiality, and an inextirpable possibility of becoming it. . . . Now one, now another principle gains the upper hand, while he is the field on which the combat is fought. Even though the one be continually victorious, still the other is continually fighting; for as long as he lives, it lives. As a human being, he is the possibility of many contrasts. Such being the case, where can inward harmony be found? In no saint and in no sinner; or, rather, a perfect saint and a perfect sinner are alike impossible. For each must be a human being: that is, must be an unhappy creature, a fighter, a gladiator on the arena of life. Painless the battle of life cannot be: it may not end without bloodshed, and in any case man must mourn; for he is at once the vanquished and the victor. *Hæc est vivendi conditio.*"

These words strike the note of genuine pessimism—that which refuses to be comforted because all effort recognizes in success its own illusions, and is pierced in its triumph by the smart of failure. Yet it is just because high aims flit before his mind's eye, because the ideal of a noble life refuses to be beaten down in the storms of sensual impulse, that he realizes so bitterly the disappointment when old memories or new hopes spoil the perfectness of the actual achievement. "The men who set before them a happy, long, and brilliant rather than a virtuous life as their aim" (he writes at Weimar, 1813) "are like foolish players who would always have brilliant, long, and successful parts; they are not aware that the great thing is not what or how much they play, but how they perform their part." And again next year we hear him groaning over the body of sin and death which drags him down: "If egoism has taken thee captive and possessed thee wholly, whether as joy or triumph, or lust or raging pain, or vexation or anger, or fear or mistrust, or any kind of envy, then art thou in the devil's claws, and the manner thereof matters not. The one thing needful is to make haste and come forth; and here, too, the manner of escape matters not."

But there is one phase of the contest between the lower and the higher self which especially exercises a fascination over his ponderings. M. Renan has recently expressed his surprise that love, which is the "mysterious thing" of all others, "the most extraordinary and suggestive fact of the universe," instead of being made by science and philosophy the principal subject of their observation and speculation, has been either passed over in silence through prudery, or disposed of by a few silly platitudes. To ignore and go round this "knot of things, this most profound secret of the world,"—is a charge that cannot be fairly brought against the author of the chapter on the "Metaphysics of Sexual Love." According to him, the lust of life, the lower life of wilful passion, has its focus and culminating point in the love of man and woman. There the lower nature has its fortalice—against which the intellect has ever to contend. Like the Greek dramatists, he finds that Erôs reigns supreme: that Aphrodite is the truly universal deity of the natural and unregenerate human being. In the attractions and repulsions of sex are found the springs of movement which guide and misguide empires and commonwealths. Its fatal powers, as a probably well-founded scandal declares, had made Schopenhauer yield to the charms of youth or beauty. But his defeat,—for so he felt it,—only served to stimulate his sense of the incompatibility between such pleasures and ideal aims. "The satisfaction of the sexual impulse" (he could write in 1815) "is utterly and intrinsically reprehensible, because it is the strongest affirmation of the lust of life." And a pervading burden of his thought is the Pauline sense of the evil present with him in the realm of night, as a den swarming with craving and despairing desires, and the anticipation of a realm of light, when the higher faculties have given us that "better consciousness" which is beyond the unrest of time.

But as his reflection turns the subject over, the antithesis between the physical and the moral grows more intense, abrupt, and uncompromising. The spirit of the ascetic, of the world-contemner, begins to govern his thoughts. He yearns—at least in half his mind—towards the vision of another world, free from the sensual and the sexual altogether. Like the man in Plato's illustration, who would fain see the hangman's corpses, he may be constrained to let his passions seek their satisfaction, but it is with a curse muttered over their loathly prey, and a prayer for deliverance from their tyranny. The very violence of his appetites whets his apprehension of the putridity inherent in a world where their every gratification is at the same time a disappointment and a degradation. No Christian hermit or Indian yogi could be inspired by keener disgust at life and its so-called pleasures, and look more earnestly away in expectation of release. He refuses, in these moods of disenchantment and penetration, to compromise with the world. A Manichean disruption between the realms of good and evil is the result of this alternation between the two poles of reflection. On one hand, lies human life and the lower world, emptied of all its idealism, reduced to its beggarly elements or naked *naturalia*, and so branded with the mark of pessimism as essentially aimless, fruitless, meaningless repetition of the same weary tale told by an idiot, full of sound and fury; and, on the other, a higher world beyond—a "better consciousness," the mere negation or abstraction from the world of common reality—an emancipation into what can only be pourtrayed as emptiness—the freedom of the dim and dark abyss in which no life is.

But, as thus appears, metaphysical problems blend with moral, and give them their characteristic form. He is equally averse to the solution of existence proposed by the materialist and the spiritualist. Against the spiritualist—by whom he means partly the theist and partly the absolute idealist—he urges the merely secondary place of intelligence in the universe. The theist sets at the head of all things an intelligent Personality, which makes and guides the cosmos, turning as it pleases, and so as merely to realize its plans, the whole movement of material things. The idealist sublimates everything into the play of thought, making the structures of the real world appear only so many knots in the skein which intellect winds out of its own resources. Schopenhauer, on the contrary, maintains that it is not a supervening thought which governs the universe, but an indwelling and non-rational nature, which only uses intellect as an instrument towards the attainment of ends it receives and tries distinctly to formulate. The centre and root of all existence is not an idea, but a nisus or effort towards being, a blind unconscious striving, which in universal movement sways to and fro, driving, yet not by preconceived ends, but by something which is not mere force and still less intellect, and is only definable as Will. That principle—neither material nor spiritual—is the silent incommunicable "One and All" of the universe, which, in animal, and, to a higher degree, in human nature, comes to apprehend itself, to transform itself into an idea, so seeing itself outwardly by reflection as well as inwardly in the deep unutterable intercourse of nature with herself. So that, in man, the petrified or hypnotized heart or will of the universe finally emerges into the light of self-consciousness. But, holding this doctrine of a real principle of which phenomena are only imperfect revelations in space and time, Schopenhauer naturally—especially in later years — came to protest no less energetically against the materialism of what he terms "absolute physics"—*i. e.*, a "physical science which professes to contain in itself the whole mystery of existence made plain." "The modern fashionable materialism," he wrote in the days of Vogt and Büchner, "can at its best explain only the shell, not the kernel of nature: for it seems unaware that the light of revelation can come only from within." Materialistic naturalism—he scornfully styles it "the philosophy of the barber's man and the druggist's apprentice"—is objectionable to him—not because of its atheism (the "One and All" is not God), not because it denies the existence of the Soul (for the Soul is only a temporary conjunction of two alien principles, Will and Intellect), but because it leaves no room for another order of being than that declared by natural science as the absolute order of existence. The belief in such an other order is what metaphysic—the ascent as it has been called from the sensible to the supersensible—seeks in its every form to inspire or justify. Hence his words: "The necessary creed of all the just and good is 'I believe in a metaphysic.'" So he writes in his chapter "on the metaphysical need of the human being."

Under the pressure of these feelings a work had been growing up in his mind since 1812. In 1814, if we may believe his own witness, "all the dogmas of his system, even the more secondary, were fixed." And as early as 1813 he wrote at Berlin: "Under my hands and still more in my mind grows a work, a philosophy which will be an ethics and a metaphysics in one:—two branches which hitherto have been separated as falsely as man has been divided into soul and body. The work grows, slowly and gradually aggregating its parts like the child in the womb. I became aware of one member, one vessel, one part after another. In other words, I set each sentence down, without anxiety as to how it will fit into the whole; for I know it has all sprung from a single foundation. It is thus that an organic whole originates, and that alone will live. . . . Chance, thou ruler of this sense-world! Let me live and find peace for yet a few years, for I love my work as the mother her child. When it is matured and has come to the birth, then exact from me thy dues, taking interest for the postponement. But, if I sink before the time in this iron age, then grant that these miniature beginnings, these studies of mine, be given to the world as they are and for what they are: some day perchance will arise a kindred spirit, who can frame the members together and 'restore' the fragment of antiquity."

This philosophy assumes its definite form under the influences of Dresden, one of the chief homes of art north of the Alps. The place is appropriate to the philosophic progeny born within it. It was the proudest claim made by Hegel on behalf of his system that in it, at length, philosophy emerged as science—as the science of sciences. It is, on the contrary, the reiterated doctrine of Schopenhauer that the pathway of reflection and abstraction, of reasoning and science, will never lead to the end which every philosophy has in view. Science has for its province the world of phenomena, and deals exclusively with their relations, connections, and sequences. It can never tell us what a thing really and intrinsically is, but only why it has become so; it can only, in other words, refer us to one inscrutable as the ground and explanation of another inscrutable. So long as our purview is restricted within these limits, and these are for us reality, philosophy is an empty word, and we are deaf to its revelations. "He to whom men and all things have not at times appeared as mere phantoms or illusions has no capacity for philosophy." This was the primary postulate of his earliest reflections, even as a lad of eighteen—the basis of his philosophy, and the root of his pessimism. But, as we saw, a like persuasion was in the very air of his youth. It was one of the phases of that idealistic faith, which, as we look back upon the end of the last century and the beginning of the present, throws a silvery light over the workers in every walk of the intellectual vineyard. Especially is it the dominant note in the theory of the Romantic school. The ideas of Tieck and his young friend Wackenroder, of Novalis and Hoffmann, are also in large measure the ideas on which Schopenhauer builds. And that idea is, that art, and especially musical and poetic art, reveals the eternal truth with a directness and power such as science cannot hope to attain. Art, they say, shows us the inner and eternal truth to which reality has concentrated itself from its dissipation among accidents and relativity—and for him who has, by art's inspiration, once seen the ideal truth of things, all particular things seem henceforth to be unreal, visionary, fugitive. "Art," says Wackenroder (in the "Heart-effusions of an Art-loving Friar," 1797), "is a seductive forbidden fruit; he who has once tasted its innermost sweetest juice is irrecoverably lost for the active living world." The road to philosophy, then, it would seem, leads through the portals of Art; and, even though Schopenhauer adds that none who have not learned Kant may enter, he, like Plato, would set the court of the Muses in front of dialectic.

"A science" (he wrote in 1814) "anybody can learn—one perhaps with more, another with less trouble. But from art each receives only so much as he brings yet latent within him. What do the operas of Mozart avail the unmusical? What do most people see in a Madonna of Raphael? And how many praise Goethe's Faust merely on authority? For art has not, like science, to do merely with the reasoning powers, but with the inmost nature of man, where each must count only for what he really is. Now this will be the case with *my* philosophy; for what it proposes is to be philosophy as art. . . . To the majority no doubt this philosophy as art will seem very much out of place. But I should imagine that from the failure of the attempt, now made for three thousand years, to treat philosophy as science, *i.e.*, according to the principles of deductive reasoning, we might historically infer that this was not the way to find philosophy. The mere capacity to discover the sequence of ideas, to combine, in other words, antecedents and consequents, may make a great scholar and savant; but it as little makes a philosopher as it makes a poet, a painter, or a musician." Like art, then, philosophy is to a large extent a private and personal possession. "There is no one philosophy existing and acceptable for all human beings. The difference in the degree of intelligence is much too great for that. The true philosophy, when it appears, will command the attention only of a few, and these, heads of the first order; though of course others may yield allegiance to it on authority, as from a sense of their incapacity they are constantly inclined to do. Beside it there will always be other philosophies for the second, third, fourth class, whereof those for the lower classes present themselves mostly as religions, in the garb, that is to say, of unconditional authority. In India, the fatherland of metaphysics, the very same thing happens. For, in the sense in which there is one mathematics and one physics for all, there cannot be one philosophy for all."

To be an artist of the first order, mere talents and erudition are not enough; and to make a genuine philosopher Genius is required. To the select few thus endowed Schopenhauer proudly felt himself to belong. To be a philosopher is to be one among myriads, and that one chosen by nature, endowed by circumstances beyond his own control, gifted by inscrutable decree. Scholars and savants may, by acquired knowledge, by the toilsome accumulations of research and erudition, make themselves a lofty position and gain the crown which science bestows upon her votaries. But the true philosopher is a heaven-born king, invested by birth and nature with the royal prerogative. His is not the method which, by slow deduction and calculation from premises of outward fact, painfully achieves some general conclusion. He is, as Novalis says of the artist, in the transcendent sense of that term—he is a magician, one who penetrates into the secret vital principle of things, and from within, by his potent wand, controls their outward movements. The genius—the great man whose life is of true benefit to humanity—is one who, unperturbed by passions and undistracted by petty detail, can see deeper than others behind the veil of circumstance and catch glimpses into the permanent reality.

A chapter in the supplement to his chief work (vol. ii. chap. 31) has been set apart by Schopenhauer for the exposition of his view of Genius. The genius has received from nature a massive preponderance of intellect above what is necessary for the demands of the individual life; a surplus he can therefore devote to universal ends. That intellect is a higher than ordinary power of seeing things—a finer, subtler, more penetrating intuition—a gift of original and almost creative perception. For its perfect development it needs to be supplemented by imagination, which enables it to see every aspect and face of its object, even those not directly presented. Whereas talent is confined to detecting the relations of individual phenomena, genius rises to a vision of the universal in the individual. But to do this it must be emancipated from the subjection in which the average man—the commonplace human being—lies to his desires and passions. The genius will therefore live a life of detachment from fugitive emotions, surveying the world in free objectivity, sober-minded and self-controlled with the gracious ease and calm of the Greek ideal of temperate will. Even while he is in the full swing and surge of sensuous emotion, he will yet, from an inward vantage-ground of calm, be able to observe himself, and, catching nature, as it were, in the act, translate it in crystallized outline into the language of intellect. And yet a genius is not—if we may so express it—always a genius; the hero cannot always be such to his *valet-de-chambre*. His very existence is a rebellion against the great law of life, is a revolt of intellect against the supremacy of will. And the will ever and anon resumes its reign, or rather the very excellence of intellect only serves to set out in clearer relief the inherent and evil contrariety of the will against itself.

Such a being is perforce a stranger in the work-a-day world. His life and conversation are in another country, a land where there is no variableness or shadow of turning; and to the crowd around him, bent on gratifying their temporal and sensual wants, he seems now to be foolish and careless as a child, now to be weighed down by an absurd and groundless anxiety. His path, although to the eye that looks from within it may prove itself equable and uniform, is, from an outside judgment, deemed a maze of folly and eccentricity. The whirl and tumults of life move on another plane; though apparently in the thickest of it, the genius, wholly rapt in higher enthusiasms, is unconscious of its interests and heedless of its designs. So-called utilitarian ends and temporal objects are not directly influenced by his doings. Hence he is out of touch with his immediate and visible surroundings, and lives, so far as temporal and visible links of association are concerned, always and necessarily alone. Without the balanced prudence which keeps in view the various relations of things, and with his eye centred on what is the chief thing needful, he is apt occasionally to attach undue significance to what the world has called trifles, and to get the name of a visionary and an enthusiast, a quixotic dreamer and phantast, a devotee of impractical ends, an isolated and paradoxical element in society.

Schopenhauer even undertakes to point out some of the physiological conditions on which the emergence of genius in an individual depends. It need hardly be added that the picture is drawn from the life; the genius is a generalized Schopenhauer. It is, in the first place, only a man who can be a genius; women—the *sexus sequior*—can at the best possess talent. The prime condition of genius is an abnormal preponderance of the sensibility, or powers of observation and perception, above the irritability and the powers of reproduction. Hence is required an unusual development of brain, a broad, high brow; but a general vigour of system and an excellent digestion are no less indispensable if the superior faculties in the machine are to do good work. From his mother the genius must inherit this brain, as well as a delicately-organized nervous tissue; while from his father he must derive a lively and passionate temperament, somatically exhibited in great energy of the heart and the circulation. A moderate stature and a short neck are especially favourable circumstances.

In the main Schopenhauer has right on his side. There is, however much men of talent may writhe at the distinction, an immeasurable distance between the mere compiler and statistician, who marshals in ordered lines and systematizes in proper formulæ the immense detail of accumulated knowledge, and the thinker who, with fresh and powerful glance, reads a new lesson in the universe, sees deeper into the secret of things, and carries up the interpretation of nature into higher levels. All true art has a charm and a glory, and is crowned by a gracious sacred nimbus which seldom falls to the lot of the worker in science. There is truth in the dictum of Aristotle, which Schopenhauer cites with approval, that poetry is more philosophical than history, that the vision of the artist soars to higher altitudes of veritable fact than Dry-as-dust by his lucubrations can attain. But when one looks more deeply, the antithesis is less clear in its issues. We may not go so far as Plato when he asserts that a quarrel of old standing separates philosophy from poetry, and that the passion-bleared eye of the poet is hardly the right medium to reflect the purest and most lasting truths. In their grandest efforts the poet and the philosopher stand close together, and the chief captains of science owe half their eminence to a touch of the poetic faculty which consummates their other endowments. Yet it seems certain that the magic and prophetic road to truth—the secret path whereby the higher revelation and the creative intuition lead their possessors to the tablelands of transcendent knowledge—is one which is often visited by the mists and fogs of illusion and self-deception, and which has often conducted those who trusted in it to the dark mountains of vanity, where they stumbled and were everlastingly lost. The true possessor of this visionary faculty is only a pioneer, and his duty is to make the way of airy speed, along which his thought shot up to the light, the king's highway for all sorts and conditions of men. The prerogative of genius is not to find out a private way of his own, a special method for *élite* spirits; but to lead the multitude, at the cost perhaps of his own martyrdom and long solitary waiting in hope, to see that the way of true genius must ultimately be the way of all. And though we cannot tell the sources from which genius springs, nor the conditions under which it appears, we may be sure that it is not independent of erudition and the teaching of history. It is not indeed any hodman of science who can see things transfigured into perfect outline by that light that never was on sea and land; but, also, it is not every claimant to the gifts of art who by a mere dictum can disclose the meaning of life. The most gifted genius works in the strength of his environment, and with the silent yet effective sympathy of his kindred according to the flesh.

A few words may be here introduced as to the chief intellectual food on which Schopenhauer was then nourished. He read carefully the works of Cabanis and Helvétius. Helvétius is the author of two works, in which, as was said, he let out bluntly the secret which all the world had agreed to keep. That secret was, that human virtue, in its ordinary phases, was at best a graceful and tasteful selfishness. "The virtuous man," he says, "is not the person who sacrifices his pleasures, his habits, and his strongest passions to the public interest, since such a man is impossible: but the person whose strongest passion is so conformable to general interest that he is almost always necessitated to virtue." Of this cynical author Schopenhauer used to say he was the favourite reading of the Almighty. He meant, presumably, that such virtue formed the favourite subject for the sarcasms of Mephistopheles in the Court of Heaven. Cabanis, again, in his work on the "Relations between the Physical and the Moral in Man," had drawn attention to the ever-interesting and ever-misleading dependence of mind on body and body on mind—the strange bond which indissolubly links together our highest and our lowest. "We conclude with certainty," says Cabanis, "that the brain digests impressions, and that organically it forms the secretion of thought."

Perhaps even more stimulating, as giving its bias to the moral and religious tone of Schopenhauer, was his introduction to the Latin translation of the Upanishads, made by Anquetil Duperron from a Persian version of the Sanscrit original. It had been published at Strassburg, in two volumes, quarto, 1801-2, under the title "*Oupnek'hat, id est, Secretum Tegendum*, &c." The Upanishads are a group of treatises which expound, with minor differences, the general system of mystical pantheism which arose as a development of the more theosophic elements in the Vedas. In their entirety they form the scriptures of the Vedānta, the primitive metaphysics of Hindostan, the inner faith or higher gnosis, which was overlaid by the fantastic polytheism of the popular creed, but which gave strength and direction to the movement known as Buddhism. To the reader of the present day, accustomed to the abundant helps which modern scholarship has provided for understanding the ancient wisdom of the East, it seems almost incredible that Schopenhauer should have struggled so successfully with this crude version by an early Orientalist, where the text (as in scholastic translations of the Arabian Aristotelians) is a medley of languages, in which original terms, deformed and imperfectly rendered, are mixed up with the Latin. . But Schopenhauer detected a kindred spirit in the rude utterances of the Indian metaphysicians, made ruder still by being twice-translated. "How thoroughly," he says (Parerga II., § 185), "does the Oupnek'hat breathe the holy spirit of the Vedas. And how does every one, who by diligent perusal has familiarized himself with the Persian-Latin of this incomparable book, feel himself stirred to his innermost by that spirit. . . . And, oh! how the mind is here washed clean of all its early ingrafted Jewish superstition, and all philosophy servile to that superstition! It is the most profitable and the most elevating reading, which (the original text excepted) is possible in the world. It has been the consolation of my life, and will be the consolation of my death."

It has been said that one undisputed fruit of the Romantic movement was its translations. Feeling around for deeper foundations, and for tried material by which to embody its plans of a new life according to nature, it went far a-field: turning into German the poetry, the philosophy, the annals of distant nations and ages. Already, in 1808, Frederick Schlegel had brought India nearer by his book on the "Language and Wisdom of the Hindoos." And Schopenhauer, while he stayed at Weimar, had made the acquaintance of another Orientalist, Fr. Majer (whose work, " Brahma, or the Religion of the Hindoos," appeared in 1819), who gave him an interest in these new regions of historical research.

In the early months of 1818, the prospective work was approaching completion, and Schopenhauer began to look about for a publisher. A mutual friend introduced him, by letter, to Brockhaus, of Leipsic. To him accordingly Schopenhauer, in March, wrote, explaining that he had completed " A new philosophical system," which he wished to get published before next Michaelmas. In confidence he lauded his wares. The forthcoming work was no mere *réchauffé* of old opinions, but a supremely coherent series of ideas, which hitherto had never entered into any man's head: a book "which would hereafter be the source and occasion of a hundred of other books, . . . clearly intelligible, vigorous, and not without beauty." For the manuscript, which was, in his own opinion, of inestimable value, and which, even from the publisher's point of view, should be worth a good deal, he asked no more than a single ducat per printed sheet, and an edition of not exceeding 800 copies. These terms were accepted by Brockhaus, and a contract drawn up, April 8, 1818. But the printers, who worked at Altenburg, did their business much more slowly than Schopenhauer expected; his impatience exaggerated the risks of delay, and imagined treachery at work; and at length he wrote to Brockhaus a letter full of bitter complaints, containing a demand that he should pledge his word of honour that, one day after receipt of the remaining manuscript, he would send the honorarium for at least forty sheets, and let him at the same time know, "with all the sincerity he could," when the printing would be finished. At this unceremonious assault on his honour and honesty Brockhaus flared up. To be told that common report charged him with dilatoriness in his payments to authors was, he said, an assertion which he must ask Schopenhauer to substantiate by, at least, naming one instance of such behaviour. As for the slackness of the press, that was no fault of his. The honorarium would be paid, in conformity with the terms of agreement, immediately upon the delivery of the last instalment of manuscript. When, notwithstanding this challenge, Schopenhauer did not think it incumbent on him to offer either defence or excuse for his charges of dishonesty, the publisher followed up his first letter by another, in which he told the author that henceforth he would hold him "no man of honour," and that he must decline all further correspondence with one "whose letters, in their divine coarseness and rusticity, savoured more of the cabman (*vetturino*) than of the philosopher." He concluded with the stinging expression of a hope that his fears, that the work he was printing would be good for nothing but waste paper, might not be realized. Schopenhauer sat calmly amid the storm he had raised, apparently unconscious of imprudence or rudeness, and firmly convinced that he had adopted the right method of dealing with a publisher. At any rate such vehemency produced its effect—for none are anxious to venture twice within reach of the bear's hug. Brockhaus urged the printer to accelerate his rate of work. The book appeared in the last months of 1818 (with the date 1819 on the titlepage), as a volume of 725 pp., 8vo., entitled "Die Welt als Wille und Vorstellung" ("The World as Will and Idea, in four books; with an appendix containing a criticism on the philosophy of Kant").

The "World as Will and Idea" is the principal work of Schopenhauer. Even more than the first of Hume's philosophical progeny, it fell still-born from the press. Like the two shorter essays that preceded it, it had few readers; and if it attracted the notice of one or two reviews, it was only as the novelty of the season, and the waves of silence soon seemed as if they had closed over its head for ever. Sixteen years afterwards (in 1834) the author wrote to Brockhaus to ascertain the state of the sales of his work. The answer informed him that only a few copies were left on hand—the greater number of those which remained unsold having been previously disposed of at waste-paper price. In 1844, when the author had reached his 56th year, he succeeded in getting Brockhaus to undertake a second edition in two volumes. The first volume, with the exception of a very few sentences interpolated here and there, is, as regards the main work, substantially a reprint of the first edition. In the appendix, on the contrary, which contains the criticism of the Kantian system, the changes are very considerable. In 1818 he had been acquainted with the "Criticism of the Pure Reason" only in the form which it had assumed in the second and subsequent editions. At a later date he had come across the first edition, and seen reason to believe that it alone expressed the genuine and unmutilated thought of Kant in his best and freest days; whereas the second edition, "to compare with it," he says, "is like a man who has had his leg amputated and replaced by a wooden one." As for the second volume in this new edition of Schopenhauer, it consists of additional or episodic chapters, dealing with special points, giving fresh instances, and touching collateral questions. He agreed to dispense with any remuneration for his labours. But even the glory he looked for was slow in coming.

The new edition went off so tardily (750 of the second, 500 of the first volume were printed), that some years after the publishers reduced the price.

All this must have been a terrible disappointment to the author, but it never for one instant made him doubt the merits of his work, or the quality of his own intelligence. Long years after he confided to one of his disciples that, upon completing the work in its first draft, he felt so convinced of having solved the enigma of the world that he thought of having his signet ring carved with the image of the Sphinx throwing herself down the abyss. And in his "Letterbag" (as he entitled one of his numerous collections of papers), the same disciple found a scrap written with the words, "That would be my highest fame if one day it were to be said of me, I had solved the riddle which Kant had given up." And in another class of papers, the so-called "Senilia," written during the last eight years of his life, he writes: "Subject to the limitation of human knowledge, my philosophy is the real solution of the enigma of the world. In this sense it may be called a revelation. It is inspired by the spirit of truth: in the fourth book there are even some paragraphs which may be considered to be dictated by the Holy Ghost."

Strange judgments have been passed on books in days past and present. They have been greeted as heavenly messages, and decried as upheavals from the bottomless pit. And no doubt there have been books which so expanded the mental horizon, and so suffused with new colour the mental atmosphere, either of individuals, or of whole periods, that after them the world seemed new-made, and those whose lot was to dwell in that later world could not even in imagination reproduce its earlier aspect. But rarely, except in the annals of religion, has any bringer of new ideas been so deeply sure of the power and truth of his visions as was Schopenhauer. The book, so he told Brockhaus, was "the fruit of his whole existence." At thirty, as he complacently generalized, the intellectual and moral endowment has reached the acme of its development: nothing afterwards can do more than slightly vary and expand a piece already fixed in its main outlines. And however such an estimate may fail of expressing the fate of all lives, it is probably near the truth in his own. "The World as Will and Idea" was not indeed the book which first made him popular—that place belongs to the fragmentary "Parerga and Paralipomena"—but it is the book which thoroughly expresses what he had to say to the world.

It is necessary, therefore, to say a little on the message which its preacher felt to be so new and precious. To omit it, would be like the play of "Hamlet" with Hamlet left out. For, one may say, there are two Schopenhauers in the field. Even the meanest of God's creatures, says the poet,

> "Boasts two soul-sides, one to face the world with,
> One to show a woman when he loves her."

Schopenhauer's beloved was no mortal maiden; but an august vision—or was it a reality?—of truth. There is the Schopenhauer of his outward biography: an irritable, petulant, paradoxical creature, plagued by a most unconquerable vanity; whose acts accuse him of being selfish, harsh-mannered, and sordid; with a history full of trivial incidents, vulgar quarrels; self-engrossed; dead to the sweet ties of domesticity, and deaf to the call of public and national interests; sinking as the years passed by into a solitary cave, whence, like the giant in Bunyan's allegory, he raged impotently at the heterodox wayfarer. Unfortunately, in some of his books, especially the later, this unpleasant self is rampant. But these same books, at their best, give the picture of another soul which, freed from the bonds of temporal quarrels and the world's litigiousness, draws close to the great heart of life, and tries to see clearly what man's existence and hopes and destiny really are; which recognizes the peaceful creations of art as the most adequate representation the sense-world can give of the true inward being of all things; and which holds the best life to be that of one who has pierced, through the illusions dividing one conscious individuality from another, into that heart of eternal rest where we are each members one of another, essentially united in the great ocean of Being in which, and by which, we alone live. A few pages, then, to complete the picture of the man, must be allowed to a brief statement of the purport of his book.

CHAPTER V.

THE book is well described in the preface to the first edition, as containing "a single thought," not a system of ideas. As time went on, the author was sometimes apt to forget this. But to forget it, is to miss much of the characteristic excellence of the work, and to neglect its essential limitations. As the exposition of a single idea, it stands contrasted with the contemporary efforts of the great systematisers. In them each branch of philosophy emancipates itself so as to be pursued, in "fancy-free" theory, merely for its own sake. Logic, ethics, and æsthetics, claim each a sphere of its own, and in the midst of one study we almost lose sight of another and of the common end. Schopenhauer proceeds otherwise. The four books into which he divides his work might, as he himself suggests, be severally said to contain the logic, metaphysics, æsthetics, and ethics of his system. But it is truer to say that they are four ways in which one truth reveals itself, in knowledge, in being, in art, and in conduct. Each aspect offers something the other was obliged to leave unsaid : but each is inwardly correspondent with the other, and expands only so far as that other permits. Each book is the complement of another: or it is its translation into a new language which brings out meanings scarcely surmised in another version. The third book, *e.g.*, is not a system, nor even the sketch of a system, of æsthetics, but rather the reflection in an æsthetic medium of moral and metaphysical truth.

The book thus expresses the vigorous, but restricted individuality of the writer. Its unity, like that of certain empires, resides in the sovereign personality which, by its intense heat of conviction, fuses heterogeneous elements into one. To this fulness of life, present throughout, the book owes its undeniable charm. The exposition sweeps along in full and massive stream, generally with a show of pellucid depth, now impetuously bearing away some obstacle, and again deviously wandering around islands, as one who lingers on his way, ever and anon touching upon the homes and interests of men, and finally losing itself on the illimitable horizons of the barren sea. Many sources discharge their supplies into its bed, and occasionally mar the transparency of its waters; and sometimes it seems as if an abrupt change of direction carried it counter to its first intent. But the underlying unity of purpose, and the palpable earnestness of tone, overcome these semblances of divergence. The style is, indeed, by no means faultless. It is often turgid, and loaded with colour. The strain is too continuous. Metaphor frequently replaces argument. But take it all in all, it is appropriate to the subject. The writer has the conviction of his message.

Unlike his earlier books, this is no purely academic discourse on a question of the schools. It is a gospel of a true life, instinct with the fervour of faith, and proudly conscious that to the vulgar it will seem the very foolishness of paradox. The young author rides forth like a knight-errant defying current idols, upturning the confident prejudices of his generation and the dominant ideas of modern civilization. The world, as his vision figures it, is drifting along a torrent which insidiously bears it, not to Elysian fields, but to an unending Cocytus of woe. The naïve dream of continuous progress to happiness increasing more and more, of enlightened peoples peacefully federated throughout the earth, are in his judgment maniac delusions : and if thinkers still arise to bid us hope the amelioration of man's estate from the wise organization of a perfect commonwealth, where equality tempers liberty and the spirit of fraternity ennobles both, these are mistaken sciolists who have failed to sound the depths—the desperate wickedness—of the human heart. Man has strayed from truth when he seeks his satisfaction in things without, in externals and accidents. Neither in a far-off God in worlds beyond, nor on the barren breast of a republic in this world, can he find safety. The things on which he has set his heart are those possessions which perish, and the knowledge, whereby he fancied he would one day learn the secret of beatitude, is only destined to increase his sorrow. Schopenhauer announces to him that life, as he understands it, is a vanity, a contradiction, an inevitable sorrow.

Nearly three centuries ago, Francis Bacon delineated in advance the career and tendency of modern civilization. The glory of man was to make the earth his servant, to turn nature into the minister and vehicle of his gratifications. To perfect that mastery of man over nature, it was indeed indispensable that man, as observer, should, by all his subtlety, strive to wrest the secret of natural processes and natural laws. But the physical sciences, which arose by carrying out this espionage, and which have gradually become an irresistible force controlling the whole conception of human life, have not unreasonably inherited the stigma of the utilitarianism they exist to minister to. To science, as to practical life, the so-called natural world has become a mere dead matter, an extended somewhat, a "body," a mere thing which is realized by being consumed. Man began by treating nature as only material for his satisfaction: and in the Nemesis of science he has himself been reduced to the level of one of the things he deals with. Science has become mechanical and materialistic. The world which it describes is a world in which there is nothing but matter and motion—nothing but simple and non-mysterious atoms submitted to changing relations in time and space.

As science—as a single factor in the great system of life—this mechanical and materialistic character has a relative place and justification. But science is not content with this subordinate position; or rather, its votaries, sunk in the dark depths of their mine, grow so short-sighted that they deny that the sun shines. They set up a materialistic philosophy—a philosophy in which physics is made absolute. Against such a philosophy Schopenhauer wages war; and in his contest he starts from the general conclusions of Kant. Kant had, with full clearness, and from a position within the ranks of science itself, raised the question as to the relation of science to life; and his answer was couched in the technical phrase that the supremacy or primacy belongs not to the theoretical, but to the practical reason,—not to the intellect, but to the will. That life is more than knowledge, is the cardinal faith which descends from Kant to his disciples, and which (it may be added) descended to Kant from Rousseau. "My philosophy," says Kant's first great pupil, makes life, the system of feelings and desires, supreme; and leaves knowledge merely the post of observer. This system of feelings is in the mind a fact about which there is no dispute, a fact of which we have intuitive knowledge, a knowledge not inferred by arguments, nor generated by reasonings which, at our option, we receive or neglect. Only this face-to-face knowledge has reality; it, and it alone, can set life in movement, because itself springs from life."

These words of Fichte serve also to mark the standpoint of Schopenhauer. The things of which science and experience predicate reality, and sole reality, are, as Kant had shown, mere appearances, divided from independent and self-subsisting being by a gulf which science, as such, is powerless to cross. The so-called realities—*i.e.*, the masses of materiality and passivity which science regards as alone existent—are, by Kant, reduced to mere ideas in our mind—or, as we may even say with Schopenhauer, to a "cerebral phantasmagoria." The world, empirically real, is, when we reflect upon it, purely and merely ideal. It is, physically or objectively considered, a picture which is due to the functions of the brain, of an organ which, through a peculiar machinery at its disposal, translates a reality which is always beyond our knowledge, into a fabric of ideas changing in place and time. Only through the intellectual function of a brain does this whole system of sense-perceived things exist.

The same conclusion had been enforced (in the earliest essays) by another mode of arguing. The great and ever-recurring feature of science is to explain by reasons, to refer to causes. Such knowledge is always and for ever relative. It never gets to the real heart of any matter: it only refers us to something more familiar or more frequently occurring. We want to know one thing, and the answer sends us to a second, and that to a third; and, in this unending throwing-back of the difficulty, we come to see dimly that, on this course, and by this method of knowledge (and it is the method of science), we can never get the satisfaction we expect. At each stage we must confess, if we are honest with ourselves, that we have remained outside the reality we profess to explore. We have only a scheme of times and places, in which we watch the transformations or successions of a reality which is as mysterious at last as at first. If we speak of forces, we are inwardly sensible how narrow is the range of that knowledge which claims to be so much. Force, which we know as matter in motion, recedes on more searching analysis into the depths of unperceived reality.

And yet reality cannot be abandoned merely because reality, as understood by science, that last and loudest prophet of modern civilization, turns out to be a mere phenomenon—a phantom of the brain. An invincible feeling assures us that behind appearance there is true being. How is it to be discovered? The early dissertation of 1813 had distinguished four species of knowledge—logic, ethics, physical science, and mathematics. In all of them we never get beyond relations between ideas. But beside and above them all there is another grade of knowledge, unlike them all, and hardly describable by the same common name. This knowledge, if *knowledge* it may be called, connects not idea with idea, but ideas with reality: its fundamental dogma—the "philosophical truth *par excellence*"—is the proposition that "my body and my will are one." Here the real and the ideal coincide. Ourselves we become aware of in two ways. Outwardly, we are, even to ourselves, an object of perception, extended in space, existing through successive times, a cause of effects and an effect of causes, a thing referred to and dependent on other things. Internally, we know ourselves by means of feeling, by the sense of muscular action, by the tone of pain or pleasure, as a system of desires, sensations, and emotions, as volitional beings—or, in brief, as Will. We feel ourselves alive and active, sentient, emotional, passionate, a surge of attention and intention, volitional and appetitive; and, as we retire into this inner consciousness, we find ourselves neither divided into parts nor suffering the lapse of time, but altogether free from the limitations of time and space.

That mysticism, which ever and anon wells up through the practicalities of Western life, speaks strongly in Schopenhauer. In the daylight of science and worldly life our existence is apprehended only as a thing of shreds and patches, a congeries of parts. We are, as it were, outside ourselves, when we adopt the standpoint of secular science: what we see is only the dead shell of our real being, the fragments into which the intellect has reduced us. Science gives but a partial view: for the intellect is itself an outsider, and has lost hold of the inner unity of life. The fruit of the tree of knowledge has served to cut us off from paradisaic immanence in reality. Culture and science have led us away from the real heart of the matter, and put us outside the grand current of existence. The intellectual life is a principle of separation and individualism. For the true apprehension of things we must, after the fashion of contemplative mystics from the days of the authors of the Upanishads downwards, retire into ourselves, and seek the secret of the universe in those depths of our own heart and will, where the distractions of sense-perception reach not. An exclusively intellectual attitude breaks up the totality into an endless series of details. But when we retire into ourselves, into the twilight of feeling, at the quiet hour when eye and ear are lulled to rest, we feel ourselves as emotion and appetite, in a word, as Will;—time and space fade away; the distinction of cause and effect is lost; we are everywhere and nowhere; in every time and no time: and, as the light of intellectual consciousness grows dim, we swoon away into the infinite.

This sense of inward reality has been deadened by the calls of ordinary life, the practice of civilization, and we have come habitually to look upon ourselves in the same materialistic way in which we regard other things. In the silent darkness of inner feeling a direct communication seems to pass at every pore from ourselves to all other things, keeping up a continuity of sympathetic influences. But in the broad light of intellect and science, things assume an isolated and independent existence. It is true that this severance and individuality is imperfect, and is implicitly denied by the power we allow to relations of cause and effect, by the essential relativity which knowledge in its every part proclaims. For everything, though professing independence, bears stamped on it a reference to something else: and that reference from grounds to conclusions, from cause to effect, is, as it were, the shadow thrown upon these separately-presented units from the unrecognized fundamental unity governing them. Philosophy comes then to reinstate in its proper influence the latent sense of solidarity through all things, which has been overlaid and lost amid the diversions and distractions of material civilization and materialistic science. And in this effort it starts from the principle of the identity, in our own individual case, between the perceived (material) body and the felt (immaterial) will.

This truth, however — the fundamental truth of this philosophy — is not a direct perception. It is rather a necessary inference by analogy from certain experiences. In the normal conditions of this life, we are never quite relieved from the sense of body as extended, as an object amongst other objects: and, on the other hand, we can never be aware of ourselves purely as will, but as first willing this, and then that. We are, in short, never completely released from the separations of time and place which reflection institutes. But there are degrees in the disruptive force of the reflective intellect, and degrees in the completeness with which we can sink into a mere sense of our identity with the moving and acting "spirit," if by that name, *pace Schopenhaueri*, we may also designate the Will; that restless appetite-towards-being, life, and realization, which sweeps through us, which we are, and which is all things. We can, at least in imagination, screw down the lamp of outward knowledge till the differentiating lines drawn by reflection grow faint, and

> "We are laid asleep
> In body, and become a living soul;"

feeling ourselves at one with

> "A motion and a spirit that impels
> All thinking things, all objects of all thought,
> And rolls through all things."

This inner self, undivided, absolute, "One and All," Schopenhauer names Will. So naming it, he implies that this truer aspect of ourselves is not a mere cognitive or intellectual power, but an acting, suffering, feeling, moving being—a force of spontaneity, urgency, and sense of effort, and not an abstract idea—an impulse, instinct and spring of life, and not a mere conception or proposition. But the absolute antithesis, which he insists upon, between will and intellect can hardly be maintained. From the will consciousness, and in some degree knowledge, cannot be wholly excluded. There must be a higher and comprehensive genus of consciousness in which the will participates. Contrasted with the consciousness of ordinary and scientific knowledge, it may be styled an "Unconscious," just as the appetites, in contradistinction from the absolutely-ideal reason, may be termed irrational. But, as so opposed, the will possesses a higher and not a lower grade of consciousness: an immediate and all-penetrating power of apprehension which defies time and space, and does not need the loitering help of the law of causality. In connection with this, may be noticed the protest which Schopenhauer made by anticipation against the critics who treat his "Will" as only another name for force. Some of his phrases, literally treated, may support the logic of this identification: but it runs counter to the whole tenor of his philosophy. The will, which is the inner reality of our body, must indeed be shorn, for Schopenhauer's purpose, of much that is attached to it in our anthropomorphic applications of it—of all associations, for example, with motive and voluntary choice. But if it is less than consciously-motived volition, it is also more than mere force: it is, to quote the vague words of a kindred speculator, "*un nisus profond, s'exerçant d'une manière aveugle dans les abîmes de l'être, poussant tout à l'existence à chaque point de l'espace.*" Apart from some analogue to consciousness, but to a consciousness *toto genere* different from the rational modes of it exhibited in the animal and human world, Schopenhauer's Will is reduced to nonentity—a mere word covering a materialist explanation of the universe by the vibrations of ponderable molecules. But if Schopenhauer does anything, he poses as a bulwark against materialism: and if he refuses to identify himself with the pure spiritualists of idealism, he is even more opposed to the mere idolaters of matter and force. His, like all philosophy, is the narrow water-shed whence opposing tendencies diverge. But, unquestionably, his main postulate is that human consciousness, when its outward powers are made to converge in a line with the inward sense of will, is the slender bridge by which we approach, so as to have at least a distant glimpse of the ultimate reality which we are, and which all other things are.

For, granting (which is much) that we can thus by a mystic process of introspection discover what we really are, the next step is to extend by analogy our conclusion to the rest of the universe. As our body inwardly seen is will, so all other objects conceal beneath their shape of extension an inner being as modes of volition. In their ultimate meaning they, like ourselves, though in different degree, are quasi-conscious energies. Thus is reinstated, under a modified form, the old belief that "all things are full of souls." Science, the handmaid of human necessities, had reduced the physical universe to a mere aggregate of extended things, marvellously complicated, played on by forces, or rather bound one to another by unintelligible, because merely external and necessary, laws of causation. Schopenhauer bids us interpret causation in terms of quasi-conscious motivation. The mystery of matter finds its explanation in terms of human consciousness: the activity, will, energy, which we apprehend as our true being is also the real being of all things. He bids us recognize, not merely in the processes of organic life, but in cohesion, gravitation, electricity, and all other types of natural energy, "our own essence, the same principle which, in our own case, pursues its aims by the light of knowledge, but, there, in the weakest of its forms, strives only blindly, stolidly, in a one-sided and invariable way—a principle, however, which, because it is everywhere one and the same (just as the first break of dawn shares the name of sunlight with the full rays of noonday), must there as elsewhere bear the name of Will."

Outwardly, then, the physical universe is an aggregation of matters, dispersed illimitably from place to place, and undergoing endless mutations in time, bound together by causal connections. The ordinary materialist sees in this a vast aggregate of realities, compared with which the human being with his intelligence shrinks into a petty thing. But the critical philosopher reverses the balance, and shows us this whole so-called material universe as a mere system of ideas in an intelligence. He points out that all those processes presupposed by the geologist and cosmogonist as taking place in infinitely distant ages, and over infinite expanses, are a description, in the pictorial language of intellect, of phenomena which, *as such*, never existed. The whole picture only exists in and through the peculiar functions of the brain :—of a partial organ of that body which the philosophy of Schopenhauer declares to be, in its inner reality, only Will. As the brain is to the whole corporeal system, so is the picture of intellect (the cerebral function), which represents reality as a wide-spread and gradually unfolded multitude of spatial objects, to the truer revelation given by the un-named and mystic organ of the undivided will. By that organ we get, not an idea, but an intense intuition, feeling, and conviction of a world which is one and all, where there is no earlier and no later, no here and there—where "a thousand years are as one day"—a world which concentrates eternities and infinities into an absolute omnipresence and unity.

Such a Will is a metaphysical—which means for Schopenhauer a supernatural — power, and wields a wizard's wand, to which time and space are nothing. The scientific instinct, with its early utterances in Bacon and Spinoza, had dismissed the doctrine of design and final causes from science to the pseudo-sciences, as they were esteemed, of theology and metaphysics. Nor, naturally, does Schopenhauer deal more kindly with a conception which, as ordinarily taught, introduces into the machinery of the world an extramundane God. But he is far from sharing the prejudice that teleology is a mere illusion, and an impossibility, because it transcends the scope of scientific causation. On the contrary, he regards it as an inadequate expression for the real unity of nature, whereby each part, without deduction by distance in space and time, immediately responds to every other. In the diverse elements of the world it is the one identical Will which disposes all beings in such sympathy that, unconsciously to the parties concerned, it makes individuals sacrifice their selfish interests for the well-being of their kind. The bird which builds a nest for offspring yet to come bears witness in its act to the omnipotence and continuity of a Will for which the interval between pairing-time and rearing-time does not exist. Nor is this all: for the chief interest of the

SCHOPENHAUER.

"One and All" of nature lies in its human bearings. Schopenhauer has a kindly eye for clairvoyance and magic powers, so far as they testify to the reality behind the veil. "Animal magnetism is," he remarks, "a most momentous discovery; it is a practical metaphysics." In ordinary experience, he admits, man's power and knowledge are restricted within limits fixed by his bodily organization. But there may, he thinks, be moments, and there may be special conditions of the phenomena, when we catch a passing glimpse of the secret supernatural intimacy that pervades all materiality :—when the *nexus metaphysicus* defies the limitations of the physical *nexus*. If we can believe (as he has tried to prove) that man and nature are only phenomenal and superficial divisions of an underlying undivided essence of will, then it is not illegitimate to suppose "a communication as it were behind the curtain or a clandestine game under the table." Telepathy, thought-reading, spiritualism, and faith-healing, become possible, and even probable. "Does one ask," he says later, "the way of the magical effect in the sympathetic cure, or in the influence of the distant magnetizer? It is the way the insect travels, which dies here, and again proceeds in full vitality from every egg that has stood the winter. It is the way in which it happens that in a given population an extraordinary increase of the death-rate is followed by an increase of births. It is the way which does not go on the leading-strings of causality through space and time. It is the way through the thing-in-itself."

Man, therefore, by the gift of intellect, has fallen from his original tranquillity in the bosom of universal nature.

He has largely lost his primal fellow-feeling with all things, and has gained instead a new organ, the intellect by which he can indirectly regain that sense of contact with other things, of which his individual existence had deprived him. Originally indeed this intellect came as a mere instrument of the will, to compensate the earlier unity of feeling. It is charged with mere will-service, to enable the will to perform what, as embodied in an individual, it finds itself less capable than formerly of accomplishing. In other words, knowledge is only sought at first under the stimulus of need, of the uneasiness of will : its perceptions, alike in animal and man, are only of things in their bearings on animal and human needs. By degrees, especially in man, the intellect rises above this immediate service to need, to a service less direct. Such service is science: where so many means are interposed between want and its satisfaction that the ultimate dependence on the will is lost sight of. So far intellect merely acts as a surrogate to supply that telepathy which the will has lost when it took individual shape. Yet, even at its highest, the scientific attitude toward things is to study them, not for their own sake, but as means for the wants of the individual, and so, dealing with them only in their outward relations, to refer them, in explanation, one to another, endlessly.

Thus, as has been previously indicated, the primary function of knowledge is to be the servant of the individual will. But, in this cosmogony, as in many others, the creature asserts himself and ends by dethroning his creator. As mere scientific idea, knowledge is for ever condemned to imperfection, and to endless finitude. It deals with individuals first, and secondly with those abstract generalizations from individuals which are the product of empirical reasoning. At its best, it but ministers to the sensualism characterizing the vulgar Will. But, probably in all, intelligence assumes a higher phase than this vulgar servitude, and is capable of a freer contemplation. Where this higher power of knowledge is fully liberated, there we have what Schopenhauer calls "Genius," and Fichte had called "Talent." Such a gifted being is the Artist, and his knowledge is the æsthetic idea. He is one who, with keen outward observation, yet has not lost his sense of universality, and has risen superior to the needs of sensuality. He sees things, not in their external accidents, but in their inner significance, their permanent value. Such a spectator looks at things as it were from inside: he identifies himself with the object of contemplation; he is no longer a needy being, one outside others, but lives habitually inspired by the sense of cosmic harmony.

Science, according to Schopenhauer, at its last step only gave us the dead abstractions it had generalized from reality. For it the individual and the general had fallen irremediably asunder. It is the glory of the artistic genius to unify what had thus been parted in twain. Art presents an individual which is perfectly representative of the universal—concentrates in a single form all the meaning that science has vainly sought to fathom by generalizing the content of a thousand single shapes. The æsthetic idea, which art thus reproduces, and which the artistic eye sees in natural forms, is something beyond the range of any mere formula to express:

no analysis can exhaust its wealth of meaning, and no collection of general terms adequately render it. Such is the splendid dower of beauty. Either in nature, or in art, it carries us beyond the individual objects to their universal and everlasting meaning; it shows us, in its special mode of delineation, that infinite and absolute being which each individual really rests upon, if he could only see deeply enough. Wherever such faculty of vision is, rich and original in genius, weak and derivative in commoner natures, it avails, at least for a time, to lull cares and anxieties to sleep, to silence the cravings of individual will, and to give us, even in the waste of this world, a brief taste of the Sabbath repose of the blessed.

To reveal these eternal significances in the life of nature and man is the function of art: and the several arts owe their characteristic differences to the grades of the existence which they in comprehensive outlines depict. The visible and sensible forms, in which the one ever-living and moving will gives itself objective existence, fall into great groups, each of which is characterized by a typical common nature. These grander grades in which the everlasting process of objectification of will into visibility and tangibility goes on—the successive scenes in that play by which the cosmic Will displays itself on the world-stage—are what Schopenhauer has styled "Platonic ideas." The lowest of them, the most elementary type of the utterance of Will into bodily shape, is the inanimate block. Hence, at the bottom of the arts stands architecture, destined to exhibit in their plain truth the play of mechanical force, the struggle of propulsion against gravity, of column against superincumbent mass. But the arts which deal more closely with man convey deeper insight into the purport of the will, and the real issues of human life. Thus, painting, under the guise of an individual figure and a single event, betrays the secrets of life and death. Its highest achievements are where it shows the individual will broken and contrite, in a state of quiescence of all desire, already tranquillized on this side of the grave. Such are the pictures of the saints who have trampled the world under their feet. In poetry, again, the highest lesson, the ethical lesson, is given by tragedy. Tragedy is a revelation to the spectator that the natural will is foredoomed by its nature to misery, and that, as one life is essentially wrapped up with another in universal will, the life of egoism is cursed, because even a victory in the inevitable struggle cannot free the conqueror from participation in the sorrow of the conquered. Lastly, music has the prerogative of representing the very ultimate essence of the life of will throughout the universe; its burden is the quintessence of all joy and sorrow—not for this or that special cause or circumstance —but as the very love of love and hate of hate.

Art is thus the interpreter of the permanent and intrinsic meaning of the drama of existence. It carries us beyond our natural selfishness and our accidental relations with other things, and lifts us out of the turmoil of sensuality. It shows that true life implies unselfishness and devotion to the truth of things for their own sake. But its lessons hardly avail save for those who have otherwise learned the secret it symbolizes. In the main its chief service is to console against the ills of life, and that by raising the eye, from immersion in particulars and their relations to human needs, to the contemplation of the essences of things.

Man, as has been seen, emerges on the scene as a being charged with individual appetites and desires, concerned with nothing but his own interests, blind to everything but securing means of gratification, wholly controlled by the lust of life, and exulting in the natural pride of existence. When his consciousness awakes, he finds himself lodged in the fabric of the body, identified with its lusts and appetites,—his intellect entirely in bondage to his passions, and without a thought beyond. If he thinks at all, it is only that he is born to receive happiness, to get his impulses gratified. He affirms that lust of life, which he finds himself practically enacting, as the law of his being. Another step, and this selfishness, which makes it his only duty to be happy, carries out its principles by reducing the whole world into a mere material and vehicle for his pleasures. In the naïve faith that he is the centre around which the universe revolves, he proceeds to treat his fellow-men and all that they consider their property, as if these were only something that might contribute to swell his convenience. Thus the selfish creed of the natural quest for happiness issues in the career of wrong—in a world of wrong-doing.

The discomforts thus arising call forth the machinery of public law, the State and its ministries of so-called justice. Civil justice, without renouncing or denying the selfish principle on which life has been based, attempts to remedy the grievances that selfishness causes, by clapping the muzzle of punishment upon the transgressing egoist. Positive law, in other words, tries to curb the lusts of egoism by imposing penalties where egoistic conduct has led to others' injury. But such secular and temporal justice has no ethical tendency, or power to reform the character. Like the whole political organization, of which it forms the central province, it seeks only to put a smiling face on things, and to prevent by its machinery of penalties the greater losses which predominant wrong would breed.

But political and penal agencies would not exert even the slight remedial influence they do, were they not reinforced by other and more purely moral stimuli. Just as vulgar science had indirectly to own the bond of solidarity which makes the universe one, so here the natural selfishness in which the cares of life entrench us from our earliest years never entirely annihilates the obscure apprehension of our essential identity with all living beings. In the stings of remorse, in the prick of conscience, we feel, as it were, the touch of the great mother of all life. Through them emerges into our waking consciousness the sense, long neglected and misunderstood, that the intervals between past and present, between individuals here and there, are only illusions of our superficial existence. As this voice of conscience is more observantly hearkened to, it serves to nip in the bud those tendencies which law sought to prune after they had fully grown. With the increase of delicacy in our perceptions of its lessons, we learn it right to renounce even what law declares our due, and find ourselves living under a new law—the law of charity and love.

Such is the supreme principle of positive ethics—the sense of universal brotherhood, or rather of underlying identity of essence. Universal benevolence, sinking self-interest in the interest of all life, becomes a never-failing fountain of virtue. This is the very euthanasia of selfishness, when the self is the great self—the supreme self of humanity, nor of humanity only—and when devotion to it means readiness to suffer for the sake of helping the weak, the unfortunate, and the wretched. Thus the will to life is purged of its bitterness when egoism becomes universalized and passes into altruism: while yet it remains true to its original creed that happiness is life's end and due. The word of the unregenerate soul was, "I am I:" but it now whispers, "I am thou," or, in the old Indian formula, "Tat twam asi:" "This art thou." With that formula on its lips, it finds the gate opened for it which leads into the heaven of optimism in its supreme transfiguration.

When sacred and pitying love has thus displaced profane and worldly passion, when individualism has been so far absorbed as to give all its goods to feed the poor, and to shelter the homeless, it might seem that the climax of ethics had been reached. But there is a further step, a negative and quietistic ethics, founded in asceticism, and justified by pessimism. Relatively the happiness of a community, or even of all sentient beings, is a nobler and truer end than the happiness of the individual; but if happiness as such is impossible, then the happiness of millions will not elevate a mere zero into a palpable amount. The service of humanity is only a delusion, unless the fruits of life really give a surplus over the costs of its maintenance. But, as Schopenhauer seeks to show in some eloquent pages, "all life is essentially sorrow." Every human existence alternates between pain and *ennui*. It is only when we confine our glance to the details of life that it presents the aspects of a comedy: "the life of the individual, looked at as a whole, in general, and noting only the salient features, is always, properly speaking, a tragedy." When this truth is perceived—that satisfaction or happiness is in this world impossible—then the final veil has been rent asunder. It is a lesson which may come, either through some shock of personal experience, or through some higher than usual power of penetrating the appearances of life. But for him who has thus seen beneath the surface of the world into the gray, cold misery of her inward struggle—who has seen the nightmare life-in-death—the service of humanity can have only a secondary charm, as a palliative of an incurable misery.

Such an one who has denied life, who has died to the body and its natural appetites, is the saint. Hitherto we have seen him only on his negative side, as the philanthropist, who lavishes on others the blessings they crave for, though in his own heart he sets little value on them. But now, girded in the panoply of self-mortification, he seeks to save himself from the body of sin and death, from the torment of an endless and manifold willbondage. His positive path—so, paradoxically, to put it,—is the path of asceticism—the religious, *i.e.*, the monastic or anchoretic life—a life which runs on a higher plane than ordinary secular virtue, and contains, indeed, the secret well-spring from which that secular virtue derives its strength. His entrance on that saintly career passes through the gate of self-renunciation — through vows of complete chastity and voluntary poverty. Keeping his body under, by a systematic course of self-repression, he sets himself free from the prison-house of life. By his own act he cuts himself away from all sensual and sensuous ties: temptations reach him not, troubles do not affect him: and though the rain and the wind bluster round him as round other men, they find him insensible. He has slain the will to life: and if to any one the will and its works (of the flesh) are all in all, then the saint lives in a world of utter non-being, *Nirvana*. With him, "knowledge only is left: will has vanished."

"The aim of all intelligence," says Schopenhauer, "is to react upon the will." But at first it seemed as if the position of knowledge were purely auxiliary. Even in the form of reasoned knowledge it could accomplish no more than to regulate and harmonize the passions, to make life systematic, and so diminish the needless friction that curtails our satisfactions. Knowledge, said the writer, could never alter character: and the dictate of wisdom, bidding us be content with being true to our own selves, advised us to gain a clear understanding of our nature and faculty, and do the best within the limits assigned to us. What we are, it was asseverated, determines inevitably what we do: *operari sequitur esse*: and inasmuch as circumstances can only modify the accidents of life, but not its essential character, it follows that knowledge can only suggest a choice of means to a pre-ordained end. Thus partial reformation is impossible, except so far as that name may be given to a choice of simpler and more consistent methods of conduct.

But total reformation is declared to be possible. We cannot amend the will. But we can end it. There is, as has been seen, a higher kind of knowledge which can annihilate it altogether. All volition is, by the pure light of knowledge, shown to be aimless, hopeless, miserable effort, and in such a vision strength comes to negate the will. How that may be done is a mystery. It would seem as if it would need a greater Will to deny this lower lust of life. But this higher Will is the will of knowledge: of knowledge which is penetrating and powerful intuition. Knowledge at first was spoken of as a mere messenger and servant of will, a substitute for the inner sympathy latent through all nature. But these latest acts of knowledge betray another origin: and show that, as elsewhere, knowledge must ultimately spring from knowledge more august than itself. The reign of Will—undisciplined impulse—blind instinct—was only the pristine stage of a will which is destined to be also intelligent. And man, as he raises himself by the process of ethical life, gradually comes to himself in the higher regions of that intellectual world, which is no mere school of words and abstractions, but freedom from the limitations of desire, and from the immersion in trivial interests of the moment. He has ascended—though Schopenhauer will not say it—from the natural to the Spiritual Will.

CHAPTER VI.

ERE his book appeared, even before he had received the final proofs, Schopenhauer was in Italy, bent on shaking off the mouldy dust left by a four years' incubation, and on plunging into the ampler and freer life with which the Northern imagination has for many centuries endowed the shores of the Mediterranean. An ineradicable longing—like such longings destined to show itself as in part only a useful illusion—has made the Germanic peoples turn again and again to the land where the lemon-trees bloom, as to the long-lost paradise where the secret of nature is still kept, and where the beauty and the grandeur of the older world still haunt the ruins of classic and early Christian civilization. Sometimes Italy has been sought as the home of Catholic art, sometimes as the museum or the burying-ground of the Italic races, sometimes as the first-awakening sleeper from the long dream in which vernacular life had sunk since the days of the Roman Empire, sometimes as the holy place of the Christian world. In these very days a young band of scholars were laying the foundations of those archæological and philological researches which have since given a new life to classical history; and a contemporary brotherhood, encouraged by the example and patronage of the enthusiastic Crown Prince of Bavaria, was reviving a sacred art, which should be pure, beautiful, and German. But it was neither with Niebuhr and Humboldt, nor with Bunsen and Rückert, nor with Cornelius and Thorwaldsen, nor with Overbeck and Veit, that Schopenhauer could sympathize. Historical inquiry, with all its paraphernalia and apparatus, he regarded as merely dealing with the accessories, the decorations, of the theatre, not with the real life. The renaissance of Christian art made him, the Hellenically and Orientally inspired, give free vent to his contempt. A shock of horror passed through the group of "Nazarene" artists and art-lovers when one day, in reply to a student who had urged against his dictum (that Greek art derived unique advantages from the clearly-defined conceptions of the twelve Olympian gods) the fact that Christianity too had its twelve apostles, he thundered out—"Get along with your twelve vulgarians of Jerusalem." And if we want to know how he felt towards the admirers of mediæval architecture, we need only read his words: "How kindly to our mind, after contemplating the glories of Gothic, comes the sight of a regular building, executed in antique style. We feel at once that this and this alone is right and true. If we could bring an ancient Greek in front of our most famous Gothic cathedrals, his remark on it would be: Βαρβαροι. It is certain that our delight in works of Gothic art reposes on associations of ideas and historical reminiscences— on feelings, in short, alien to art. In them we no longer discover that pure and complete reasonableness, in virtue of which every item admits of strict calculation, and even itself lays the calculation bare to the intelligent spectator—a reasonableness which characterizes the antique architectural style. In Gothic we have what is merely arbitrary. Hence its mysterious appearance; we have to suppose aims unknown, secret, inscrutable; hence its mysterious and hyperphysical character. In architecture, the Gothic style is the negative pole, or it is the minor key. . . . In the interests of good taste, I should be glad to see large sums of money expended on what is objectively, *i.e.*, actually, good and right, and intrinsically beautiful, not on what derives its value merely from an association of ideas. When I see this sceptical age, then, so actively building the Gothic churches left incomplete by the mediæval Ages of Faith, it seems to me as if they wanted to embalm deceased Christianity." Clearly a pagan like this could only be a "disturbing element among the comrades" of the æsthetic crucifix, and we need not be surprised to hear that his own countrymen, freshly fervid with the aspirations of the patriot, the scholar, and the Christian, were not the people with whom Schopenhauer companied most smoothly and often in Italy.

Many of those who sojourned in Italy at this date, treated it as a country which, bereft of all national life of its own, was good enough to serve as the Vauxhall and Cremorne of those who had grown tired of the cold respectabilities of Northern Europe. It was the land of love and song, a land where the aspects of life and manners were more picturesque than elsewhere, where woman was, if not fairer, at least more lightly responsive to the tones of passion, and where conventionalism seemed to vanish with the Northern surroundings amid which it had used to be supreme. At this very date Lord Byron was in Venice, drinking the wine of life to the lees, gathering, in a city which had lost all larger interests, the materials for the cynical pictures of "Don Juan," and soon to find himself enslaved to the charms of the Countess Guiccioli. And Byron, like Schopenhauer, even more so, cared little for the historic past of Italy or for the archæology of art. The gorgeous remains of Byzantine Christendom at Ravenna did not elicit from him a single word. Few things, he said, had made so fast an imprint on his mind as two monuments in the Certosa at Ferrara. *M. L. implora pace: L. P. implora eterna quiete.* "These two and three words," he says in his letters, "comprise and compress all that can be said on the subject. They contain doubt, hope, and humility; nothing can be more pathetic than the *implora;* and the modesty of the request,—they have had enough of life; they want nothing but rest; they implore it and *eterna quiete.* . . . I hope whoever may survive me, and shall see me put into the foreigners' burying-ground at the Lido, within the fortress by the Adriatic, will see these two words and no more put over me."

On the 1st of November, 1818, Schopenhauer was in Venice, probably unheeding and unaware that, on the 22nd of the preceding month, Hegel, then forty-eight years old, had begun his lectures at Berlin. The stranger threw himself with zest into the customary relaxations of the place; and the place cast over him the full spell of its enchantments, so that, even in later years, he could not recall these days of fading autumn without a burst of soft emotion through his whole soul. Byron, apparently, he did not meet, except perhaps to catch a passing glimpse of him one day as their gondolas crossed on the way between Venice and the Lido (where Byron used to take his morning ride). After a few weeks in Venice, he was off by route of Bologna and Florence to Rome. There he spent the winter, engaged in the study of Italian, especially Petrarch, and, though not a connoisseur, paying diligent attendance on the art-collections. At the theatre and opera he was all his life a frequent visitor; not to go to the play, he would remark, is like trying to dress without a looking-glass. His main social intercourse was with Englishmen; his own compatriots, prepossessed against him by unfavourable gossip from Berlin and Weimar, were not likely to be conciliated by his shyness, his eccentricity, and his paradoxical airs.

Indeed, hardly a keener contrast can be found than between the mood in which Schopenhauer visited Italy and that which made Goethe freely expand in the stimulating environment and throw himself on observation of the humours around him. Schopenhauer gathers notes in a "Travel-book"; but, instead of being a record of observations, it is a diary of moralisings and of subjective moods. Of the Italians he only notes that they are shameless, alike in their audacity and their baseness. Catholicism seems to him a mode of begging one's way to heaven, instead of earning it by honest work. Pictures and statues serve him to confirm the judgments on man's life which he had just set down in his book. At Bologna he notes that the sense of one's own want of worth is not only the greatest, but the only real pain of mind; "such an almighty consolation is the lively knowledge of one's own value, and therefore to be preferred to every earthly blessing." At Naples, whither he had proceeded in March, 1819, he congratulates himself on his work achieved, and anticipates the monument which posterity will raise to him. It was at Naples that a letter from his sister first gave him some news of the publication of his book. Goethe had glanced into the book (averse as he was by nature to introspection), and had picked out two passages as especially to his liking: the first, pp. 320-21 of the first edition (Book iii. § 45), where Schopenhauer holds that the canon of beauty is at once in the mind and in the object—as it were an *à priori* anticipation by genius of the "idea" which nature goes out half-way to meet him with; the second, pp. 440-41 (Book iv. § 55), where he points out that the true wisdom of life is to be true to our own selves. This and other letters of his sister remonstrate, chaffingly and seriously at once, with him for misanthropy, a disposition to parade atheism and cynicism, for scoffs and skits at Germany and German ways, and express a romantic sisterly interest in love passages of which her brother talks in his usual hardened infidelity.

In May, 1819, he was at Venice on his return. At Milan, a letter from his sister reached him of very unwelcome tenor. It announced the bankruptcy of the Dantzic house, in which, attracted by a good rate of interest, his mother and sister had invested almost their whole means. Schopenhauer, who had only 8,000 thalers in the same peril, at once replied that the little he had left he was ready to share with them. But his tone changed when he heard that his mother and sister had agreed to accept the bankrupt's composition of 30 per cent., to which the other creditors had also signified their assent. For this precipitation, betraying as it seemed to him the usual womanish incapacity for the management of business, he could not forgive them; and when his sister urged him to join in the general discharge, suspicions so poisoned his mind and envenomed his words, that an eleven years' silence fell between him and the two other members of his family. He determined to stand out for all or nothing, and carried out his purpose with a well-conceived procedure which proved that he had inherited no small portion of the mercantile spirit and legal ability of the Dantzic merchants, if they do not even suggest a strain of the old Dutch tenacity which had kept out the sea and the Spaniards. An old family friend advised compliance with the adversary while yet he offered terms. But Schopenhauer, with an *Et tu, Brute*, to the faithless counsellor, and an inflexible front to the enemy, declared that, though he would not offer any active opposition to a composition with the other creditors, he could not accept the mere bagatelle offered; but, as he was not immediately in want of money, and the bills were not due, he would let them lie till it met the convenience of both parties to have the debt discharged. His father's honest and hard-won earnings, which were his *par Dieu et son droit*, he would never condescend to accept as a grace from another. The utmost he would descend to was to give a full discharge if 70 per cent. of the sum due were paid instantly. "I can imagine," he concludes, "that from your point of view my behaviour may seem hard and unfair. That is a mere illusion, which disappears as soon as you reflect that all I want is merely not to have taken from me what is most rightly and incontestably mine, what moreover my whole happiness, my freedom, my learned leisure depend upon;—a blessing which in this world people like me enjoy so rarely that it would be almost as unconscientious as cowardly not to defend it to the uttermost and maintain it by every exertion. You say, perhaps, that if all your creditors were of this way of thinking, I too should come badly off. But if all men thought as I do, there would be much more thinking done, and in that case probably there would be neither bankruptcies, nor wars, nor gaming-tables." In the course of the summer of 1821, the agreement of the rest of the creditors with the Dantzic firm, A. L. M. & Co., was signed, Schopenhauer, according to compact, making no overt opposition. But immediately after, August 27, 1821, he sent in the first of his three bills, accompanied by a letter which showed the firm he had them in his hands. His method was successful; within ten months all his three bills were paid up, with interest, to the amount of about 9,400 thalers. It must be added, however, that about half of the sum thus recovered was a few years afterwards again lost, in consequence of what turned out an imprudent investment in Mexican bonds.

The narrative of this two years' struggle for right between the solitary scholar and the commercial firm will be read with mingled feelings. In a world like ours, every assertor of rights who stands to his guns against chicanery, delinquency, and superior force, must be counted a friend of mankind. No one can refuse a tribute of admiration to the indomitable resolve and combative acumen of the defendant's claim; and there will be some to sympathize with his parting shot to the defaulter in these crusty words: "Your children will still drive past me here in dashing equipages, while I, an old outworn college teacher, pant and wheeze upon the street: and so long as you are not in my debt, I say 'God bless them.'" But there are other sides to the picture, besides the capture for once of the crafty fox. When Schopenhauer, with a claim amounting to about one-fiftieth of the total liabilities of the firm, stands aside and lets the other creditors close their losing bargain, with the remark, as he puts his tongue in his cheek, that it is no matter of his at all, one's respect for the wisdom of the serpent is modified by a few deductions for the strain of hardness. It is perhaps even more painful to see the angry suspicions darted against his sister. Yet, in explanation, and therefore in extenuation, it has to be noted that this promptness to suspect evil is a fundamental trait of his temperament. Evil fancies rose easily in his head, and painted disaster impending at every corner. The very heads and tips of his pipes were kept under lock and key; and he never committed his chin to the barber's razor. His valuables were even so successfully concealed that, in spite of the Latin directions contained in his will, it was difficult to find some of them. The same desire for baffling impertinent curiosity, or worse, made him latterly keep his account-books in English. And all this was not merely because, being of Hamlet's mind, he thinks that one can "smile and smile and be a villain." It was rather that he was haunted by a vision of a pauper old age—the vision of

> " Cold, pain, and hunger, and all fleshly ills,
> And mighty poets in their misery dead ; "

and, in the force of that preponderant craving for independence and competence, magnified every incident that seemed to threaten his future by depriving him of the dividends which were to be his mainstay.

The same alarms suggested other projects during these two years. At Heidelberg, where, on his way from Italy, he spent the month of July, 1819, the plan of becoming a university lecturer (*privat-docent*) suggested itself to him, and in Dresden, whither he went next to set his belongings in order, after a year's absence, he still pondered the suggestion and sought for information on the comparative chances of success at Göttingen, Berlin, and Heidelberg. But those were days in which the seats of learning laboured under the suspicion of being the homes of a radical and revolutionary spirit. Ever since the great bonfire at Eisenach in October, 1817, when a gathering of German students had triumphantly consigned to the flames various symbols of coercion and reaction, and especially since the murder of Kotzebue by a theological student called Sand, in March, 1819—on the charge of having betrayed the holy cause of German freedom to the interests of the so-called Holy Alliance—the Austrian and Prussian governments had set on foot a system of espionage and repression against supposed anarchic or insurrectionary tendencies. The so-styled "Karlsbad decrees," ratified by the diet, September 20, 1819, led to a vigorous *Demagogenhetze*, or "baiting of demagogues," throughout Germany, and especially in the Universities. In these circumstances it was clearly incumbent on every candidate for an official post to purge himself from all taint of "demagogy," and to confess himself a quiet and loyal subject. Schopenhauer, therefore, writing to Professor Lichtenstein as to prospects of an opening at Berlin, is careful—in a characteristic way—to disown all sympathy with political heterodoxy. "What I am and have for long been engaged in, and what, considering my nature, is the only business I can be engaged in, are things which concern humanity equally at all times and in all countries, and I should look upon it as a degradation if I had to direct the serious application of my mental powers to a sphere which to me seems so small and narrow as the present circumstances of any one time or country. I am even of opinion that every scholar, in the higher sense of that word, ought to cherish these sentiments, and leave to statesmen the reform of the machine of State, just as the statesman should leave to him the higher and more perfect knowledge. I have a most extremely low opinion of those *soi-disant* philosophers who have turned publicists, and who, by the very act of seeking a sphere of direct influence in and on their contemporaries, clearly own themselves incapable of penning a single line posterity would care to read." Evidently the Romantic Liberals would have even less ground to bless Schopenhauer than they had in the next year to count upon Hegel after the blast in the preface to his " Philosophy of Law."

The result of Schopenhauer's inquiries was to make him decide on Berlin, and, after going through the needful preliminaries (consisting in an application to the dean of faculty, presentation of specimen copies of his published works, and a lecture delivered *in consessu facultatis*, with a sort of *viva voce* examination following) he began his career as *privat-docent* by offering a course of lectures, six hours a week, on philosophy in general (*doctrina de essentia mundi et mente humana*) in the summer session of 1820. Already, in the *viva voce*, he had had the satisfaction of an encounter with Hegel, and the pleasure of fancying he had tripped the great professor, and he chose as his lecture-hour the precise time at which Hegel's principal course was given. He flattered himself apparently that he would carry everything before him. His talent for monologue in conversation seems to have been considerable, and this no doubt led him to fancy that oral exposition would be his strong point. But students are undoubtedly a race with ways and likings of their own, and success as a lecturer is not always to the wisest, ablest, or best of thinkers and teachers. The fact stands that his course was a failure ; it collapsed before the close of the term. His notice-paper, it is true, at the beginning of each session reappeared on the boards: but the lectures, which even at first drew only a "scratch" audience, were never again actually given. The competition of men like Hegel and Schleiermacher was no doubt difficult to contend against. But when Schopenhauer, like some others of his unsuccessful contemporaries, attributed his failure to the machinations of the arch-enemy Hegel, and to the all-prevailing poisons which he dropped into the ears of Altenstein, the minister who dispensed academic patronage, he was simply giving free play to his proclivity to groundless insinuation. Not unnaturally a number of capable but self-conscious teachers, contending in the dark against each other for place and pay, in an atmosphere quivering with political feverishness, will see plots and stratagems weaving all around them. But, when we read the specimens of these lectures which his disciples (not altogether honouring their master's expressed opinions) have published, we can partly explain how he missed the reputation of a popular lecturer. It may be conceded, perhaps, that in any case the doctrines of his book would hardly have supplied the proper material for the educational functions of a professor. But, apart from that, his style wants the directness and simplicity which befits the academic chair, and with its somewhat rhetorical quality seems more calculated to interest a general audience of fairly educated people than a class of professional students. To write a good book and make a good lecturer require two very different sorts of ability. Possibly, too, an audience expects one who addresses them to take a less oracular and lofty attitude than was in Schopenhauer's manner.

But Hegel was not the only victim of his suspicions. A colleague and contemporary, rather younger than himself, F. E. Benecke (subsequently a philosophical writer of some repute), had reviewed his book in the *Litteraturzeitung* of Jena, and, in the course of his notice, had put in inverted commas passages which were not in the text *totidem verbis*, but more or less judiciously compounded constructions by the reviewer out of the actual words. Schopenhauer was furious. First he called upon the editor to insert an acknowledgment of the inaccuracy of the quotations : next, receiving no reply, he charged the editor with making himself a virtual accomplice of the forger : next, at his own cost, he inserted in the journal for February, 1821, under the heading "Necessary Censure of Falsified Quotations," a paper in which Benecke was roundly accused of a "slanderous lie." The angry author felt sure there was more in the article than met the eye : that it was the work of a rival, anxious to undermine his credit and ruin his prospects of an audience, or of promotion. Thus, alike with colleagues old and young, he was on bad terms. Even his studies, devoted at this period to such doubtful branches of science as electro-magnetism and cerebral physiology, do not seem to have flourished. To society he was almost an utter stranger, and we need not too curiously pry into his amusements. That he was ill at ease, and his temper unwholesome, the following trivial trouble will show.

At the very time, August, 1821, at which he began to see land in his long dispute for capital and interest with the Dantzic firm, a new worry of litigation laid hold of him. His lodging was at No. 4, Niederlagstrasse (not far from the Crown Prince's palace), in the house of a widow, named Becker, where he occupied two rooms, in front of the door of which was a small *entrée*, or hall, common to him and a neighbouring lodger. In this hall, he had, as he complained to his landlady, once found three stranger women engaged in a conversation, and the landlady assured him it should not occur again. But on the 12th of August, as he returned home, he again found three women on the spot, whom he, in the absence of his landlady, at once requested to withdraw. Two of them made no objection; the third, a sempstress, who occupied a small adjoining room at the head of the stair, declined to comply. A few minutes later Schopenhauer re-emerged from his room, walking-stick in hand, and, finding the sempstress still on the same spot, again asked her to be gone. Upon her refusal, he took her by the waist, hauled her out, throwing her things after her when she cried for them; and, when she, almost immediately, returned to fetch something she had still left, he again, but this time violently and using an offensive epithet, pushed her forth, so that she fell and made outcry enough to alarm the whole house. On the following day, the sempstress, Caroline Luise Marguet, aged forty-seven, laid her complaint before the court, alleging, in addition to the above facts (which seem to have been practically admitted by Schopenhauer), that he had torn her cap, kicked and beaten her, and left on her person the marks of his violence. The offensive epithet alone he admitted to have been in fault: for the rest he held he had only defended his rights as a lodger. After a lapse of six months the case was decided in his favour. The complainant thereupon appealed. On hearing of this step, Schopenhauer, who conducted his own case with the same lawyer-like skill, on the whole, as he had already shown in other conflicts, sent in to the court an application to have the affair settled before May, as he expected to start about that time for a trip to Switzerland and Italy. Naturally the court could only ignore such a request: and in his absence he was sentenced to a fine of twenty thalers for slight injuries inflicted.

He, meanwhile, was off to the Alps, and after a few weeks among the mountains descended, in August, to Milan and Venice. The winter of 1822–23 he passed at Florence, and in spring passed farther south. In May, 1823, he was back at Trient, and in June had returned to Munich, where he spent about a year, apparently in loneliness, and for the latter part of the time in ill-health. Throughout the tour, indeed, he was mainly on his own resources, and, when he did join in the casual society which the traveller finds, it was to English people rather than his own folk that he turned. In fact, from this time forward he generally used English in his account-books and in his solitary monologues, read English newspapers, and preferred English articles for domestic purposes. Readers of his later writings will notice the frequency with which he quotes incidents from *The Times*. Of what he did or saw during this period there is practically no record. All correspondence between him and his mother or sister had ceased since the close of 1819. There are, indeed, the manuscripts of his "Travel-book" and "Letter-pocket." From these we learn that the traveller is much in harmony with the adage that there is no new thing under the sun; only the shape and colour of the animals in distant lands is new: their inner principle is the familiar "Will to life." At Schaffhausen the tourist rediscovers that "a sublime melancholy of mood, in which we have a lively and intimate conviction of the worthlessness of all things, of all enjoyments, and of all human beings, and therefore crave for nothing and desire nothing, but feel life as a bare burden, which must be borne to the not very distant end, is a far happier mood than any state of longing, be it ever so cheery, which puts a high value on fleeting shows and makes an effort to catch them." At Trient it is re-affirmed in the note-book that "the will in man has exactly the same purpose as in the animal: to be fed and to beget children;" with which, perhaps, we should remember the language of another passage from the Italian note-book: "'Temples and churches, pagodas and mosques, in all countries and from all ages, in splendour and grandeur, bear witness to the metaphysical appetite of man, which, strong and inextirpable, follows hard upon the physical." And at Gastein, to which he removed in May, 1824, to take the baths for his health's sake, he consoles himself with the reflection that "the best the world has to offer is a painless, tranquil, tolerable existence," and that the "surest means not to be very unhappy is not to desire to be very happy." In August of this year he is back at Dresden, apparently in better health and spirits. Plans of new work pre-occupy him during his nine months' stay there; amongst others, an idea of translating Hume's works into German, as an introduction leading up to his own system, and as a counterblast to the systems then current in Germany. He even wrote a preface to the projected work; but the project itself went no farther.

At Berlin, to which, notwithstanding his dislike of the place, he returned in May, 1825, his first business was to clear off arrears in the case with the sewing-woman, which, during his absence, had assumed a new phase. She had subsequently alleged more serious injuries than she had at first complained of, and made a demand for aliment on the ground that the final effect of the fall had been permanently to incapacitate her for work. Accordingly, while Schopenhauer was enjoying his holiday in the city of Giotto and Dante, he had received notice that his property had been arrested, where it lay, at Mendelssohn and Fränckel's bank. In October, 1824, he was condemned to pay five-sixths of the costs of the suit, charged with a mulct of forty-one thalers for outlays, and ordered to pay the woman fifteen thalers a quarter as aliment. Upon his return to Berlin he did his best to get the verdict reversed; but the decree was made final in March, 1826, from which time up to her death, twenty years afterwards, he had to charge his accounts with a debit of sixty thalers per annum. On the certificate of her decease he then inscribed the epigrammatic words: *Obit anus, abit onus.*

The reader may think it was hardly worth wasting so many words over this wretched little episode. And yet, in the paucity of biographical material for the twelve years between 1819 and 1831, one is obliged to keep one's eyes even on the fluttering of the little straws which show how the wind blows. The emptiness of all human interest makes even a quarrel in the police-court a stirring incident. After all, the incident throws its light on the coarse and passionate nature of the man, which gives a taint of meanness to what was probably after all a justifiable assertion of right against impudence. One underlying moral, not very far off anywhere in Schopenhauer's life, is that if life is to be tolerable at all, we must not rend asunder too rudely the delicate web of ideal sentiment which, age-defying and ever fresh, forms the natural garment of reality. And another is that few natures, if any, are not much the worse from a course of isolation, which, with no restricting duties and no encouraging hopes, leads them to speculate on life at a distance whence it appears cold and heartless, as the planets, which "through optic glass" the eye sees only as a desolate enigma, a region of the shadow of death. At this date, too, Schopenhauer, the noonday height of life passed, felt as if his youthful enthusiasms had been swallowed up in the sands of disappointment. As in summer, after the bright effulgence of June is ended, there sets in awhile a duller season, a stagnant colourless time, in which the eye pensively regrets the blossom and the verdure, and cannot in imagination anticipate the rich though sobered flowers of autumn, so in man's life a presage of death and a sense of vanity sometimes come as a revulsion after the first burst of adult life. Schopenhauer had had his times of visiting by that sweet spirit of passionate love, which, rightly served, makes twice glad the voyager of life, whether on sunny sea or in wintry storm,—wrongly ministered to, makes the career fruitlessly expend itself on "shallows and miseries."

His earliest love-poem had been in 1809 evoked by the charms of an actress, ten years older than himself—Caroline Jagemann, a favourite of the Grand Duke of Weimar; he had even (if we may trust a daring legend) told his mother that he would gladly take her to his home, even though she were but a stone-breaker on the highway. When he came out as *privat-docent* in 1822, a wife had sometimes risen in his fancies as the obligatory complement to the expected professorship. Later on, he dreamed of marrying and settling in a country town, where the household economy would not be endangered by the temptations of running up a long bill with the bookseller.

But, in the meanwhile, he grew more and more into the confirmed old bachelor, to whom his dog is dearer than a wife. In a letter of his sister's, in 1819, she expresses a regret that "in his one letter there were two love-stories, without any love." To one who thus played at love without love, it is hardly wonderful that the only lesson gained from years of intermittent amorous experience was cynical indifference to the sex. By that fatal gift of detachment of which he was so proud—his special *kniff* (trick)—a "high degree of cool-headedness, which suddenly and instantaneously could drench with the coldest abstract reflection, and so preserve in crystallized form the liveliest perception or the deepest feeling which a lucky hour had brought"—he was only the better enabled in this case to penetrate to the cruder bodily elements of life, and see either the animal or the corpse instead of the living woman nobly planned.

Woman, in his judgment, having been by nature

destined solely for the duty of child-bearing, occupied in Western Christendom a totally false position, which was largely to blame for the restless struggles of civilization. Her life, culminating in a few years' sudden burst of charms, solely in the interest of the species, leaves her otherwise a perpetual child, needing guidance and tutelage, incapable of being ruled except by fear, and hence a constant mine of danger. Morality, strictly speaking, she has none; save an unreasoned weakness for compassion. Essentially unjust, all women, some openly, others in secret, hold that what they call love emancipates from all moral obligation, all claims which established conventions may have asserted to the contrary. The beauty with which they are credited is even unreal: as a matter of fact they are, when coolly observed, an ugly sex; and all their charms are really an illusion due to the potent spell of a physiological attraction which intelligence and reasoning are powerless to dissipate. In the whole matter of love, man, the lord of creation, is but the victim of natural law and metaphysical agency; while he deems that he pursues his own pleasure, he is but an instrument on which Nature plays the melodies accordant with her general scheme. That such a being as woman, devoid of all originality in art, science, and literature, should, in the monogamous systems of Europe, be raised to a position of equality with man, if not of superiority, is to Schopenhauer's mind a serious mistake, pregnant with all those fatal consequences which the annals of wedlock persistently exemplify.

With views like these it would have been a wonder if Schopenhauer had taken a wife. To descend to her meaner pleasures, to waste precious hours on frivolity, and to be sure that faithlessness and rivalry are the natural drift of her temperament, is a prospect of disaster not lightly to be incurred. Deliberate antagonism, however, is in one way preferable to indifference ; and woman was certainly a pre-occupying interest in Schopenhauer's mind. A strongly sensual nature like his, bereft of the proper counterbalancing checks in constraining work and many ties, would naturally brood over the problems of sexuality. There were amongst his papers notes, (written in English,) on love and matrimony, from the periods 1819-22, and from 1825-31, couched in a forcible plainness of speech which rendered them unfit for publication. For on these, as on other matters, he prided himself on absolute truthfulness to himself—on self-confession. A record of this self-confession—this outpouring of the heart's scum which the Catholic penitent is sometimes accused of offering to God through the priest—Schopenhauer drew up with like accuracy for himself. To such a manuscript, entitled 'Εἰς ἑαυτὸν (after the well-known soliloquies of Marcus Aurelius), there were references found in an annotated copy of the "Parerga," in vol. ii. § 58 (about horse-chestnuts and Spanish chestnuts), and vol. ii. § 322, apropos of hypochondria. On applying to the executor (Schopenhauer's biographer, Dr. Gwinner), the legatee (Dr. Frauenstädt) to whom these books had fallen was informed that the manuscript in question had been burned, in accordance with its author's last oral directions, and with the approval of another friend and disciple. The notes, declared to be unsuitable for publication, were stated to contain prudential maxims, favourite passages, matters referring to private relations to certain persons, and in general only *personalia*. Gwinner appears to have used them sparingly in the preparation of his biography; otherwise they have gone—probably not much to our loss, so far as knowledge of the man is concerned, and much to general gain, so far as they might have suggested the motives for philological dissertation over unsavoury details.

And so Schopenhauer, his anxieties painting in dark colours the difficulties which a married man with little fortune and no gift for regular work might have to contend with, continued to philosophize and to remain single. His warmest welcome was at an inn; his chief acquaintances those he met at the table of the Hotel de Russie. He read much at the Royal Library, was a *habitué* of theatre and concert-room, and solaced himself with his flute. Yet various projects for finding an open door into the realms of popularity occupied him. At one moment he fancied that, though he had lost the day at Berlin, Heidelberg might yield a more promising ground for philosophic teaching. He made himself acquainted with Spanish, and was thus enabled to draw largely on Calderon. He took the opportunity of getting a Latin version of his "Theory of Colours" inserted in an optical *corpus*, and hoped that, thus clothed in the common language of scholars, it would engage a wider circle of readers. But he was doomed to be disappointed. The copies he directed to be sent to three English men of science received no acknowledgment. But Schopenhauer was not to be daunted in his confidence by repeated failure. Assured of the truth of his message, each repulse only made him seek a new point of attack; every moment of darkness prolonged only prompted him to scan the horizon more narrowly for a glimpse of the light that must and would come.

Thus, in December, 1829, after reading an article in *The Foreign Review and Continental Miscellany*, in which a wish had been expressed that England might ere long have a translation of Kant, he addressed a letter (under cover to the publishers of the review) to the writer, offering to undertake that task for the "Criticism of Pure Reason," the "Prolegomena," and the "Criticism of Judgment," at the rate of about £2 3s. a sheet. As a specimen of his workmanship he enclosed a couple of pages translated from Kant's "Prolegomena" (§ 13, Note 2). That work he looked forward to completing within three months; the "Criticism of Pure Reason" would occupy a whole year, if the translation was, as he wished and intended, to be really well done. With these explanations of his plans, he asked the writer of the article to help him towards finding a publisher. In addition to the mere translation he proposed to give a few annotations, for, as he added (the letter is in English), "Sterne made a prophetical pun, saying, in 'Tristram Shandy': 'Of all the cants which are canted in this canting world, the cant of Criticism is the most tormenting.'" He introduced himself to his correspondent as a "teacher of logic and metaphysics," and as the author of a system of philosophy which "has not attracted the general attention in the degree I expected and still I think it will one day do." In less than three weeks he had an answer from Mr. Francis Haywood, the writer of said article. That gentleman explained that he would prefer to be directly and nominally responsible for the translation himself, receiving corrections from Schopenhauer, and dividing with him the net profits arising from the publication. This, of course, was far from suiting Schopenhauer's views, and his next communication was sent direct to the publishers of the *Foreign Review*. To them he suggested that, if they felt themselves unable to form a judgment on the proposal, they might do well to consult the " very sensible and clever gentleman who wrote the analysis of Novalis, and that of Jean Paul's works in your Review, if only I was sure that not he too, like Mr. H., will have more in view his private interest than the good of literature." He went on to urge, with great truth, that "a century may pass ere there shall again meet in the same head so much Kantian philosophy with so much English as happen to dwell together in mine." The publishers, in reply, assured him that he had misunderstood Mr. H——, and hoped that something might yet come of the proposed union of translators' forces. But they do not appear to have made any use of the suggestion to take counsel with the "very sensible and clever gentleman" who, as everybody knows now, was no other than Thomas Carlyle. Even so, Schopenhauer had not yet shot his last bolt. Next year (1831) he wrote to Thomas Campbell, the poet, in somewhat the same terms as he had employed to Haywood. The occasion of such an application to Campbell, who had many schemes for promoting the interests of literature and education, was that he had lately urged the formation of a club by which authors might manage and protect their own concerns. But this letter has no further history; whether the friend, who was to hand it to the poet and certify Schopenhauer's knowledge of English, failed to perform his task, we know not. Thus ended in failure a proposal which might have had unexpected results; and Kant's *Kritik* had to wait till 1838, when a translation appeared by the very Francis Haywood we have heard of. But it seems as if Schopenhauer had, during these years, been smitten with a passion for translation—a craft which, as he conceived and sometimes exhibited it, is one calling for the nicest scholarship, tact, and ability, instead of being, as it is too often supposed, a piece of unskilled labour which any hireling or novice may make bold to undertake. His account-book for March, 1830, contained an entry of a fee of 22th. 12sgr. "for translating the prophet of St. Paul's," whatever that may have been. Not long after he projected (but did not immediately execute) a translation of Balthazar Gracian's "Oraculo Manuel y Arte de Prudencia," a work somewhat in the style of the French aphoristic moralists. The translation was published by Frauenstädt in 1862.

In the summer of 1831 the cholera, which had appeared in Russia the preceding year, visited Berlin with a severe attack. Amongst its victims was Hegel, who was carried off at the beginning of the winter session. Schopenhauer, who, like the Italian pessimist, Leopardi, was constitutionally a man of terrors, took flight at the approach of the plague, and in early autumn sought refuge in Frankfort-on-the-Main. But "fate and supernatural aid" counted for something in this move. His philosophy, as we have seen, leaves open a wide door for the entrance to and from the other world; mystic influences, magical summonses, wraiths and warnings, all can find their way through the inner avenue from the ever-real to the variably-apparent. This is how he describes the event in the roll of manuscript he entitled "Cogitata." "On New Year's night, between 1830 and 1831, I dreamed the following dream, which signifies my death in the present year. From my sixth to my tenth year I had a bosom friend and playmate of exactly equal age, who was called Gottfried Jenisch, and who died whilst I in my tenth year was in France. In the last thirty years I can have thought of him but very rarely. But on the said night I dreamt I came into a field, not familiar to me; a group of men stood on the field, and among them a grown-up, tall, slender man, who, I know not how, was made known to me as that same Gottfried Jenisch, who bade me welcome. This dream had much to do with making me leave Berlin upon the entry of the cholera, 1831; it may have been of hypothetical truth, a warning, in short, that, if I had remained, I should have died of the cholera. Immediately after my arrival in Frankfort I was the subject of a perfectly distinct apparition, as I believe, of my parents, and signifying that I should survive my mother who was still alive; my father, already deceased, carried a light in his hand."

CHAPTER VII.

WHEN Schopenhauer left Berlin, it was in the first instance only to seek a temporary asylum from the pestilence. Berlin, it is true, had long been hateful to him; but its evils were at least dulled by familiarity. The change of scene only made him more acutely realize his isolation, and brought on a fit of depression. In his gloom old memories came back, and the fancy struck him to reopen correspondence with his sister. Adele, who had only been waiting for such an opportunity, at once responded, and, without going back on bygones, told him how she and her mother had quitted Weimar, on grounds of health and economy, and settled at Bonn. From Weimar, indeed, the glory had departed; in the new order of things which followed the treaty of Vienna, it could not hold the place it had in freer days maintained. Both mother and daughter, however, continued to develop the literary style that had grown up under the influences of Weimar society. Adele, like her mother, became an author: her works being a collection of stories founded on popular legends, in 1844, and a novel called "Anna," in 1845. They are said to show taste and grace, rather than power, and to evince considerable skill in narrative. Brother and sister seem to have had many points in common. Adele, like him, found herself a stranger in life—felt herself cut off from any real intimacy with those around her—and sometimes thought death would not be an unwelcome release from a world that was for her so much an empty show.

The correspondence thus resumed was a few months later extended to include their mother. She was still the same, and her first words in reference to her son's low spirits consisted, with a little friendly *badinage*, in advice not to succumb too readily to the misanthropic proclivities of hypochondria. It was, perhaps, unfortunate for the efficacy of such counsel that it came almost simultaneously with the news that the agent who managed their common property at Ohra had died, leaving his accounts largely in arrears. Yet though the silence that followed the family estrangement was now broken, these advances did not lead to closer approximation. Schopenhauer moved on in his solitary way.

In the course of the summer of 1832 he made the experiment of changing his domicile from Frankfort to Mannheim, to which, in the beginning of winter, his books also were transported. The claims of the two cities as places of residence were carefully weighed against each other—an operation the business-like character of which is shown by a table of their respective merits and demerits that was found amongst his papers, drawn up, *in English*, on the cover of an account-book of the period. From this table it appears that, notwithstanding the superior social advantages of Mannheim, its more intellectual and artistic circles, "a nicer table in later years," a "better foreign bookseller," and "more consideration," Frankfort carried the day, on the ground of its advantages of climate and situation, "better plays, operas, concerts," "the gaiety of the place and all about it," "an able dentist and less bad physicians," and "more Englishmen." "You are more at large, and not so beset with company given by chance, not by choice, and more at liberty to cut and shun whom you dislike." In June, 1833, accordingly, decided by this experimental test, he returned to Frankfort, never again to leave it, except for a few, and these not very extensive, excursions, up to his death, twenty-seven years later.

Thus, as it might almost seem by accident, he drifted into what was to be the haven of his rest. From the merchant "free cities" of the north, Dantzic and Hamburg, where his youth had been chiefly spent, he passed, after a varied experience of Thuringia and Berlin, in his later years to the great market city of Western Germany, itself quasi-republican like his birthplace. He was now forty-five years of age. At that epoch in life the stormier passions have probably been brought under control, and the age of reason, if ever, has come, when a man's guiding spirit has learned to make its best possible inner kingdom out of the materials of temper, faculty, and circumstances of which it has the disposal. For better or worse, his manner of life runs henceforth on even rails. If he be a bachelor, especially, the events of one day probably repeat with stereotyped regularity those of another.

It was certainly a lonely existence, but not devoid of compensations and happiness of its own. "The first forty years of our life," he says in one place, "supply the text; the next thirty add the commentary." And that commentary afforded not a few grounds for self-congratulation. Some losses there were, of course, to record. "In the blossoming-time of my mind, when the brain had its most vigorous spring," he writes, "whatever object my eye might touch upon uttered revelations to me, and there rose up a series of ideas which were worth writing down—as written down they were." But, on the other side, against youth is scored the memorandum that "an augmented intelligence has for its immediate condition a heightened sensibility, and for its root a greater vehemence of will." With advancing years, experience and philosophy had enforced the conviction that the Will is the element of vulgarity in man, that the passions are the stigma of our affinity with lower natures. "There is no safer test of greatness," he remarks, "than the faculty to let mortifying and insulting expressions pass unheeded, and to ascribe them, like many other mistakes, to the weakness and ignorance of the speaker —merely, as it were, perceiving, without feeling them."

> "Therefore I summon age
> To grant youth's heritage,
> Life's struggle having so far reached its term,'

says Ben Ezra in the poet. And Schopenhauer, comparing past with present, notes certain defects in the early days.

"Youth," he notes, "has in general a certain melancholy and sadness, while age is cheerful." The young man is over-stimulated by the variety and complexity of the world; his imagination makes it promise more than it can ever perform; and thus he is for ever burdened with longings and yearnings, depriving him of that tranquillity without which happiness is impossible. These predispositions are aggravated by the influence of works of fiction, which, with tissues of false presumptions and vague unreal theories of life, pervert his whole future career. That career he expects to meet in the shape of an interesting romance. "In my years of youth," he confesses, " I was delighted when my door-bell rang, for I thought, now *it* would come; but in later years, my feeling on the same occasion had rather something akin to terror—I thought, there it comes."

"A chief lesson of youth should be to learn to enjoy solitude—a source of peace and happiness." Before the age of forty, each should have experienced the truth that what makes the weal or woe of life is, not what he possesses, not what he ranks at in others' opinions, but what he intrinsically is in intellect and character. By that time—especially if he be one wrought by the special handicraft of the great artist of nature, and not a mere manufactured article in the common shop—he will scarcely be free of a certain touch of misanthropy. And in the sixties the impulse towards solitude becomes a really natural and even instinctive one. The young man, therefore, should learn betimes how to be alone, not to be dependent on chance company to cure his *ennui*, or need to roam the globe to escape the reproach of his own meditations. He should learn to be at home, and at ease, with himself. An intellectual life protects not only against listlessness, but against its attendant evils. It is a bulwark against bad society, and the many dangers, disasters, losses, and expenses into which one falls in seeking fortune in the real world. "My philosophy," he sums up, "has never brought me anything in, but it has spared me very much."

His chief consolation, then, is philosophy—"a plant which, like the *alpenrose*, or the *fluenblume*, only flourishes in free mountain air, but deteriorates under artificial culture." Not, indeed, as he emphatically adds, the philosophy of sophists, charlatans, obscurants, who falsify and stunt knowledge, and, least of all, of that arch-sophist who (he roars aloud) has corrupted the very organ of knowledge, the understanding itself. But (and here his voice takes a milder tone) "a philosophy which is no church and no religion. It is the little spot on the earth, accessible to but a very few, where truth, everywhere else the object of hatred and persecution, can at once find release from all constraint and oppression, can, as it were, celebrate its *saturnalia*, which permit free speech even to the slave, can even have the 'prerogativa' and the first word, rule absolutely alone, and let no other hold sway beside it. The whole world and everything in it is full of design (*Absicht*), and of design mostly low, common, and bad; only one place is certainly free of it, and lies open to intelligence (*Einsicht*) alone."

During these later years the daily life of the sage of Frankfort passed according to a regular scheme, of which his admiring disciples have left a minute programme. Between seven and eight o'clock, winter as well as summer, he left his bed, and sponged himself in the matutinal tub, taking special care to bathe his eyes.

His housekeeper had orders to keep to the kitchen all morning; so after he had prepared his own cup of coffee, he settled down to work during the forenoon—those three, or more rarely four hours, when he found his brain freshest, and which he held long enough for any student who really thinks as he reads or writes. Except after eleven o'clock, to accommodate a friend or admirer, and that more frequently as years roll on, these hours exclude all interrupting visits. At noon, a signal from his housekeeper reminding him of the lapse of minutes, he stops work, diverts his mind by half an hour's relaxation on his flute, and then dresses. At one o'clock he dines in the *Englischer Hof.* Of the company at the *table d'hôte* he does not think highly. It was noticed that for some time he had each day put down on the table a gold coin, which he afterwards replaced in his pocket, but it was not easy to guess the import of the action. It turned out that it was in consequence of a wager he made to himself to pay the sum over to the poor-box the first day the officers dining there talked of anything besides horses, dogs, and women. Schopenhauer's idea was probably not original: a book of sketches of travel (*Bilder aus Helvetien,* &c.) by the poet Matthisson, published in 1816, tells the same story of an Englishman at Innsbruck in 1799. But occasionally, if a suitable hearer presented himself, he would launch out in grand style on some of those subjects which he had thought over and made his own; and when these monologues occurred the guests hardly knew where to look, in amazement that topics of intellectual interest should be discussed in a *salle à manger.* Dinner over, he returned to his rooms, refreshed himself with coffee, and, after an hour's siesta, gave a little while to lighter literature.

For he was not one who cared much to season the banquet of life with personal talk, or even with that more decorous and dignified phase of personal talk called history. Yet, as he reminds us, "there are two histories: the political, and that of literature and art. The first is the history of the will; the second of the intellect. The record of will is from end to end distressing, even terrible: agony, want, deception, and horrible murder, *en masse*. The record of intellect is everywhere gladsome and cheery, even where it has to describe aberrations. Its chief branch is the history of philosophy. This is in fact its fundamental bass, which rings even through the other history, and which, from that fundamental position, serves to mould the opinions which in their turn rule the world." Books, after all, are the truest friends; among which he has special favourites. His much-loved Petrarch he ranks before all the other Italian poets; Ariosto is frivolous, and Dante too scholastic and grotesque. In German there is much worth reading; but it is neither in the early epics, nor in the productions of the day. Of German style the truly national characteristic is its clumsiness. An admirer of Shakespeare and Calderon, he has not the petty spirit which is blind to national weakness; thinking, indeed, that no man who himself stands high can fail to be most distinctly aware of the faults of his compatriots, just because he has them nearest and o'tenest in view.

Of the literary style of his contemporaries he is scornfully critical, especially of the mutilations to which they subject the German language, largely, he believes, from the low commercial motive of economizing in syllables. With malicious pleasure he draws out long lists of the ways in which the so-called scholarly world mangles the graces of its mother tongue. Partly he attributes this to a false idea that one should try to write exactly as one speaks. The true author, rather, having in view a sempiternal public, will not let himself down to the fashion of the hour, but adopt a statelier style. But the great cause of the degradation of style comes from the neglect of classical training. To imitate the style of the ancients, says Schopenhauer, is indispensable for one who would become a great writer. By writing Latin, for example, one learns to treat writing as a work of art, the material of which is language. "Without Latin, indeed, a man must be content to be counted amongst the vulgar, even though he be a great virtuoso on the electrical machine, and have in his still the radical of fluoric acid." Nor is this all. There is no more inspiring diversion for the mind than the study of the ancient classics. To take one of them in one's hand, were it only for half an hour, is to feel refreshed, relieved, purified, elevated, and strengthened, exactly as if one had drunk from a fresh spring in the rock. Not that Schopenhauer is above a romance, if it is genuine. There are four he names as the foremost of their species, "Tristram Shandy," the "Nouvelle Héloïse," "Wilhelm Meister," and "Don Quixote." And they owe their rank to the fact that, art being a sort of *multum in parvo*, which, with the least possible expenditure of outward life, brings the most vigorous movement in the life within, they all, on a slender background of incident, unroll a rich portraiture of the acts of the soul.

About four o'clock Schopenhauer, still in dress-coat (of an unchanging fashion) and white neckcloth, started for a "constitutional." By the help of description we can picture the stout, broad-shouldered, and rather undersized old gentleman, with beardless chin (in later life, he had come to think beards indecent), over-full mouth, ample and furrowed brow, bright blue eyes, deep-set and widely parted by a broad nose tending to aquiline, and with the suspicious look of the partially deaf. In these strolls his regular companion was a poodle, one of a succession (varying in their colour) which had shared his room and board since student-days at Göttingen. About the year 1840 and later it was a white one, and went, as special favourite, by the name Atma (the world-soul of the Brahmins); from 1850 to his death, a brown poodle, called Butz. Of this dog he was very fond, noting its looks and movements with philosophic eye, and so attentive to its wants, that if, for example, a regimental band passed the house, he would get up in the midst of an earnest conversation, in order to put the seat by the window in a convenient position for his little friend to gaze out. The children of the neighbourhood soon came to know the poodle, and when they came home from their play on the Main-Quai they would, among their other experiences, recount to their parents how they had seen "young Schopenhauer" sitting at his window.

But this fondness for his dog was only an instance of his general tenderness for the animal world. To his mind the spirit of Christendom is condemned by its treatment of animals. The ruthlessness with which a Christian populace (he remarks) kills, mutilates, and tortures creatures aimlessly, and with a laugh,—with which it strains, in his old age, the last energies of the horse, the beast that has served it so long—cries aloud to heaven. One would almost fancy Schopenhauer had heard the retort of the ignorant Italian peasant to one who blamed his maltreatment of a creature—"*Non è cristiano*": and one is tempted to suppose that the prohibition against the use of dogs for drawing vehicles at Frankfort (revoked since the Prussian annexation) had some unknown connection with the philosopher's ideas. But while he denounced men as the devils of the earth, and pitied the animals as its tortured souls, he had no patience with those who contended for "mercy" to the animals. What they want, he replied, is not mercy, but justice: they who, in all essentials, are the same as man. Blumenbach, as he recalled, had, when lecturing at Göttingen, restricted the use of painful experiments on animals to cases where great issues of science were at stake. But nowadays, he said, with flashing eye, every miserable medical student in his torture-chamber claims a right to inflict on animals the most horrible torture, so as to decide problems the answers to which already stand in books he is too lazy or too ignorant to poke his nose into. But Schopenhauer, unlike many who strain at the camel once in a century and swallow the gnat every minute, felt even for the pangs of the dog on the chain, and the bird in the cage. "The lover of animals knows," he adds, "that, even in their case, the deep pain, caused by the death of a being who has been our friend, springs from the feeling that in each individual, even an individual animal, there is something ineffable, something unique, and of which the loss is irretrievable. Ask one who has accidentally dealt mortal injury to an animal he loved, and who has had his heart torn by the pain he felt at its parting look."

Sometimes, though rarely, a young friend would be admitted to share in these walks. Away they rushed along the streets, the dog gambolling ahead or loitering behind, till his master summoned him with his whistle. Schopenhauer had a theory, which he fortified by the authority of Aristotle, that a couple of hours' rapid movement daily was essential to health; and so, even in the summer heats, he would tear along at a pace which his companion found it hard to emulate. A traveller from the opposite direction might, perhaps, as they passed, diverge to the left; whereupon, with a scowl, and in a voice loud enough for the offender to hear, Schopenhauer would remark: "Why don't the blockheads turn to the right? An Englishman always turns to the right." If the sarcastic fit was on him, he might even treat his companion to a mimicry of the clown's lumbering movements, and remark that stolidity and silliness imprint their stamp on every limb and gesture. Yet, at other times, the misery of a beggar might call forth his unstinted charity. His stick, meanwhile, a short stout cane, thumped the ground vigorously at every step. Sometimes, even when alone, he would suddenly halt under the arrest of an idea, look about him, and again hurry on, with some half-articulate exclamation, which a passer-by might fancy to be an injurious epithet. As at length he got beyond the region of streets (Frankfort then numbered less than 60,000 souls), he would strike for a quiet path, and stop, perhaps, now and then to admire the landscape through his eyeglass. When with company, he would talk continuously, even while walking rapidly; but he generally walked alone, and then his lips were kept religiously closed.

After a two hours' walk, he paid a visit to the reading-room, glancing regularly at the English *Times* and any magazines or reviews he had access to. But if he made good use of the daily and periodical press, he was far from blind to its faults. The newspaper, he would say, is the seconds-hand of history. Not only is it of less noble metal than the two others: it seldom goes right. In the so-called leading articles, which play the part of chorus to the drama of contemporary event, exaggeration is as essential as it is upon the stage. The point of them is to make as much as possible out of every occurrence. The extravagance and caricature which thus arise make newspapers and other journals a permanent source of contagion to style in literature : and Schopenhauer would not be sorry if the State could see its way towards establishing a censorship over their language. The anonymity which they nearly all encourage breeds a lying and disingenuous spirit, which affects the form no less than the matter of their utterances. They drag down literature to the level of vulgar passions, and it is through them that the spirit of the age, which, like a bitter east wind, blows through everything, finds its way even within the precincts of art and literature.

From the reading-room he often betook himself to the play or to the concert. If it was a piece of good fortune for the aged still to retain their love of study, it was also well, he thought, to keep an open heart for the artistic side of life, and a certain susceptibility to outward things. Especially music: for if the eye is the sense of the *understanding*, the ear is the sense of the *reason*. Music is a language which all alike comprehend, —a melody to which the whole world is the text. Its raptures, however, are only fully to be enjoyed when heard in the mass or the symphony: in the opera the music is harassed by the burden of a meaningless piece and doggerel verses. His growing deafness latterly deprived him of the full appreciation of these pleasures; but he might often be seen listening with closed eyes to a symphony of Beethoven, and was known occasionally to leave the hall after such a piece, rather than wait to let the impression be effaced or vulgarized by meaner minstrelsy. Between eight and nine, he took a cold supper, generally by himself, sipping a half-bottle of light wine. On returning home, he generally read for an hour, smoking, as he did so, an ell-long pipe. He retired to bed early, and allowed himself a long night's rest; for a thinker and writer needed, in his opinion, a longer than ordinary time for recuperative inactivity: and whereas in general his rule of life, like his philosophy, was modelled on the lines of Kant's example, he regarded Kant's early rising as a wanton waste of vital energy, avenged by the dotage of his declining years.

Whether such a life was the happiest he could have had is a question unprofitable to discuss; it certainly cannot be said that it was either misspent or unworthy of a philosopher. For such a temper and such an estimate of life as he took, it was apparently the wisest course. Nor is it much to the point to say, as has been maliciously insinuated, that it was far removed from the ascetic ideal he had so highly glorified. He himself repels the suggestion that the philosopher is bound to realize his own great ideal more than other men. "It is as little necessary that the saint should be a philosopher as that the philosopher should be a saint; just as there is no necessity for a perfectly beautiful human being to be a great sculptor, or for a great sculptor to be also a perfectly beautiful human being. It is a strange requirement to insist that the moralist shall recommend no other virtue than he himself possesses. To reproduce in conceptions, abstract, universal, and distinct, the whole essential being of the world, and in these permanent products of reason to preserve its image and reflection always at disposal,—this and nothing else is philosophy."

The point at which Frankfort-on-the-Main gave special impetus to his reflections seems to have been furnished by the societies for the prosecution of natural history, physics, and geography, which were established there shortly before his settlement in the town. At any rate, the first break in the silence he had maintained since 1818 was his publication, in 1836, of a small book, entitled, "On the Will in Nature," and described on the title-page as "a discussion of the corroborations which the philosophy of the author has since its first appearance received at the hands of empirical science." To discover and accumulate such corroborations had in fact become almost a "fixed idea" with him. Whatever he read, or heard, or saw, passed at once in his mind through an alembic heated by the intense conviction in which he held his central dogmas. And it appeared to him that an incredulous and careless age would be most likely to listen and believe, if he could show that certain of its own scientific prophets had been occasionally led on to utterances which resembled his own. In that case physics, starting from its terminus, has arrived at a point where it meets with metaphysics; and in the confirmation which the teachings of either method both give and receive, "the two sets of investigators must feel like miners in the depths of the earth, who, from opposite points, are bringing the two ends of a tunnel to meet, and who, after they have long worked in subterranean darkness, trusting to compass and level only, at last experience the long-expected delight of hearing the blows from each other's hammers."

Of the eight or nine chapters which make up the book, and all turn on his metaphysical theory, that on "Physical Astronomy"—to which Schopenhauer himself attributes special merit—may serve as a sample of the method. The essay comments upon a text furnished by a passage in Sir John Herschel's Astronomy, published in 1833 in the "Cabinet Cyclopædia," which at present stands as follows (the words in square brackets being inserted in later editions): Chap. viii. § 440: "All bodies with which we are acquainted, when raised into the air and quietly abandoned, descend to the earth's surface in lines perpendicular to it. They are therefore urged thereto by a force or effort [which it is but reasonable to regard as] the direct or indirect result of a *consciousness* and a *will* existing *somewhere*, though beyond our power to trace, which force we term *gravity*." On this not very promising substratum he proceeds to develop that metaphysical doctrine of the essential paramountcy of the will—which, as has been often noticed, is so hard to reconcile with his ethical doctrine of the supremacy of intellect. "In my view," he says, "the eternal and indestructible element in man, what therefore constitutes the vital principle in him, is not the soul, but—if I may be allowed a chemical expression—the *radical* of the soul, and that is the Will. The so-called Soul is a compound, the conjunction of the will with the intellect. The intellect is the secondary, the *posterius* of the organism on which it, a mere function of the brain, depends. The Will, on the contrary, is primary, the *prius* of the organism, which depends upon it."

Yet even so, the public would not have his metaphysics at any price: the book made but few converts. "Nathless he so endured," and undismayed offered to vindicate Goethe's colour theory for Poggendorff's "Annalen," and gave advice to Rosenkranz anent his edition of Kant. Even in his own town, where he was better known as the son of the celebrated authoress, Johanna Schopenhauer, than for his personal merits, he ventured, "in the interests of Goethe and good taste," to address a memorial to a civic committee which sat to consider the plan of a monument to the greatest of Frankfort's sons. This memorial laid down the principle that a bust is the only statuesque monument suitable to the heroes of letters, and that the shortest inscription is the best, and then with considerable detail suggested the general conception of a work in bronze. The civic committee of course knew better than to accept what it regarded as the eccentricities of a mere scholar and amateur.

In 1838 his opportunity seemed really to have come. The Scientific Society of Drontheim in Norway had offered a prize for the best essay on the question, "Whether free-will could be proved from the evidence of consciousness." The subject was, as it were, cut out for him; his performance was soon ready; and in February, 1839, he heard that it had won the prize, and that he was elected a member of the Society. It seemed at last as if he heard the shouts of applause from the long waited-for crowd approaching to hail his triumph. To the Society he wrote a Latin letter, thanking them in his lucid and graceful style for their kindness, and asking to be allowed to publish in Germany, not later than the following year, his essay, which, as he said, had been composed *con amore*, and contained thoughts on which he had pondered long and made frequent notes—"things to last for this and for many a year." His request, which he had expended much ingenuity in showing to involve no loss to the Society, was granted. Meanwhile he was engaged in the composition of a second essay, in competition for another prize, offered as long ago as 1837 by the Royal Danish Academy of the Sciences at Copenhagen, for a discussion of the sources or foundation of morality. So confidently did he look for victory, that in the envelope containing his address he enclosed a request to the Academy to expedite the news of the award by post, and a statement that he proposed to publish the essay along with that accepted at Drontheim. It was a terrible shock when the Danish Academy made known its decision that the one essay (Schopenhauer's) which had been offered in solution of the question, "Whether the source and foundation of ethics was to be sought in an intuitive moral idea, and in the analysis of other derivative moral conceptions, or in some other principle of knowledge," was unworthy of the prize, and that on three grounds: first, that the essay contained no adequate examination of the bearings of metaphysics on ethics; second, that the arguments, adduced in proof of compassion being the root of morality, were weak; and third, that several of the chief philosophers had been contumeliously dealt with. The last article—as if the *summi philosophi* were to be held sacrosanct and inviolable—was too much for one who already regarded himself as a *summus philosophus*, the true heir to the succession of Kant's throne, which had been usurped by these babblers, sophists, arch-deceivers, and humbugs. From this time his rage against the accursed three, Fichte, Schelling, and Hegel, is only tempered by withering contempt for their wretched henchmen, the professors of philosophy, and by lordly pity for their infatuated dupes. There was, he felt sure, a plot to ignore him, to bury him in silence, to shut him, the true prince and rightful heir, like a Caspar Hauser (a half-witted creature whom political fanatics for a while claimed to be the disinherited heir of Baden), in the dungeons, and to secure for the vile pretenders the continued enjoyment of academic sovereignty. But suppressed he would not be: and his motto henceforth was war to the knife and no quarter. His writings from this time forth are perpetually exploding in invectives. The names of Hegel and Fichte, and, in a less degree, of Schelling, are like the red rag to the angry bull. It is undoubtedly the fact that the works of these thinkers do not so lightly commend themselves to the vulgar intellect as his own; and for those who have not the capacity or the training requisite to appreciate them, it is the easier course to pooh pooh them with the usual epithet of transcendental nonsense. An acute, but prejudiced critic, like Schopenhauer, stimulated at once by the natural antipathy to alien modes of thinking, and by the jealousy of an unsuccessful competitor, had no great difficulty in fastening on the weak points in his adversaries' systems. Nor, if he had contented himself with this criticism, or with the demonstration that many of the loudest advocates of these systems merely followed a fashion, and had not got more than a new weapon of dialectic, would he have been outside the mark. Unfortunately a disproportionate sense of his own ability and honesty, assisted perhaps by his isolation and self-involved ruminations, led him to arrogate over other philosophers rights of judicature which no human being can claim or safely exercise. It was through these promptings of vanity on an able but biassed mind that every author in philosophy who did not allude to his services, or who disparaged or criticised them, was liable to be splashed with dirt from a very ample vocabulary of abuse. Even a friend who diverged was apt to be visited with mild contempt, and a hint to study once more in their integrity the utterances of the grand Lama of Frankfort on the subject. "I dread silence about my system," he confesses, "as a burnt child dreads the fire;" but he is not more tolerant of speech, unless it be inspired by the respectful allegiance of a disciple. His works, he hints plainly to some of those devoted followers who could not stifle an occasional hesitation, are even as a Koran, which, rightly studied and commented upon by the illustration Sura throws upon Sura, is able to make wise even unto salvation.

The two ethical treatises—one which had, and one which had not carried off the prize—he published in 1841 at Frankfort, under the title of "The Two Fundamental Problems of Ethics." These two problems are the freedom of the will, and the basis of morality. The discussion is little but an expansion of some pages in his principal work. Freedom of Will, if taken, as generally happens, to mean a denial of the law by which act and volition depend upon motive with the regularity characteristic of causal sequence elsewhere, is, he decides, a chimera. In the phenomenal or empirical field, consciousness, when interrogated, shows that on a given character motives have a predictable result. But free-will, if thus eliminated from the realm of observation, is, after Kant's example, re-instated in the metaphysical world, *i.e.*, in the real sub-conscious world which the intensity of self-knowledge discloses in our own will. The Will, in its original self-hood, is above and beyond the forms of causality. In the mysterious region where our character is ultimately formed, we are our own creators. When we consider ourselves re-absorbed in the bosom of undivided reality, we find we are, and, as it were, make, that original will, which, by the light of consciousness, we discover as our irrevocable character, as the principle of action out of which, on the stimulus of occasion, flow the thousand acts and volitions which in their successive aggregation gradually reveal what manner of beings we are. We are free, in short, because in the sub-conscious or supra-conscious life, we are each to ourselves that omnipotent and originative Cause, which, according to the theistic doctrines, rules over us from without as a transcendent providence, directing us as if we were mere puppets in his hand. Thus in the inaccessible reality into which we can—as by faith—transport ourselves, we find the source of our responsibility. It is to our real selves we are responsible. The act, which, from one point of view, flows by necessary sequence from a character unalterably fixed, is seen from a higher standpoint to be the continuing affirmation of that eternal act of self-assertion or will-realization, which is carelessly spoken of as it had been already once for all accomplished. We are still, metaphysically speaking, responsible, *i.e.*, free in each single act, because it is the same timeless self which wills and acts to-day as willed and acted of yore.

On the question of the original or derivative nature of morality, Schopenhauer parts company from all who teach "heteronomy," or the reference of the moral judgments to the law and sanction of an external authority. Amongst these he takes the liberty of including Kant: for the reasoning power which, according to Kant, is the source of the moral law's unconditional command or categorical imperative, is alleged by Schopenhauer to be a merely nominal disguise of the Divine law. Reasoning, taken alone, he holds, as he had from the first held, can only apply by deduction what has been otherwise established; it has no original or indefeasible right of its own to issue commands. Where then are we to seek the original form of that law which reason administers? Not in God, and not in Society and the State. The only conception of God he admits is a transcendent God, "the God of the Jews": and no fiat of authority, even of omnipotent authority, can ever transform might into right. As for political society, all it can do for morality is to restrain wrong-doing by the terror of its penal sanctions. For whatever else it may effect, it requires the co-operation of something *within* the agent it seeks *outwardly* to control. The sanction and source, standard and criterion, of morality must be an inward principle, a real and vital fact in the human being. That principle Schopenhauer discovers in the feeling (however faint or "unconscious") of solidarity between individual and individual, the sense of brotherhood pervading, though unnoticed, all the generations that share in animated life, a self-same metaphysical substance which makes the whole world one kin. Beyond the egoism which the conditions of individual life foster, and beyond the selfish "love" which craves only for the satisfaction of selfish appetite, there is an altruism, absorbing selfishness and losing self in the totality, a longing which provokes to self-sacrifice, self-denial, and unselfish love. It may count for little in the phenomenal sphere, where the storm and stress of life silence its utterances. But when the schooling of adversity has taught the foolish, and the eagle eye of wise genius has seen through the vanity of selfish life, these truths are heard and appreciated. It is on this latent sense of the ultimate identity of one and all that morality is founded. That sense or feeling ethics clothes in abstract language, and without such underlying sense the theory would only be a vain attempt to lay on man a foreign yoke—the yoke of a God whom he knows not, and of a society which could be no more than a despot. Man, therefore, is metaphysically, if not physically, a moral being: and it is to that inner being—transcendent to his outward observation though not to his inward experience—that the moralist appeals.

"To preach morality is easy; to find a foundation for morality is hard," had been the motto of the essay. The ethics of Schopenhauer is no concealed appeal to cupidity, no roundabout proof that it is more politic to be moral. It does not seek to persuade, still less does it command. Morality, it says, is your inmost nature resting on the laws of your metaphysical being, which in ordinary consciousness you forget. In the heyday and frolic of life you roam about the world, sucking the sweets of existence, self-absorbed, and forgetful of others except with a view to making use of them. The moralist opens your eyes to your place and surroundings. But morality is after all only a principle of mediocrity. It can help, perhaps, to burst the bonds which cut you off from union with others. It can teach you—what your natural endowment prepares you to feel—that you are only a fragment in the great organism of life. But it does not gu iar enough to reveal the delusion of life altogether. To accomplish *that*, morality must be transfigured into the religion of an inner self-denial which annuls also the world of vanity in which that false self resides.

Three years later (in 1844) appeared the second edition of "The World as Will and Idea," from which, as the fruit of twenty-four years' study and reflection, he hoped at length to win the long-delayed recognition of his worth. It seemed at first as if even these hopes were destined to failure. The change in the public temper and judgment was tardy. And yet a change was gradually taking effect. The reign of Hegelianism had come to an end, about ten years after the death of the founder, by the secession of the abler and more ambitious students who had learned its methods. Even from the first it had never been so solidly founded as a superficial view suggested, but had to contend with the suspicions of religious orthodoxy, and the tendencies of specialist inquiry. Its strength lay in that high-souled idealism which had descended from the age of Revolution, and which, though, after the War of Liberation, in 1815, it lent itself to the service of the existing organization, yet never forgot its first-love—the realization of truth, beauty, and righteousness. But, as time went on, there arose a new generation which found itself unable to accept the identification of the real and the reasonable—which set the individual in utter antagonism to the state, and determined to burst asunder the chains of authoritative tradition. Historical inquiries, and especially researches into the origin of the creeds of the Church, took the place of attempts to rationalize and adapt to the use of present intelligence the beliefs of the established *régime*. But besides the disintegrating force of the historical inquirer, with his philological and archæological criticism, other influences were active, and foremost among them the immense increment in the power and scope of the experimental sciences, following upon the growing attention to material progress. An ounce of fact was held worth tons of theory; and enthusiastic young scientists, like Schleiden, animated by the spirit of Macaulay's notorious essay on Bacon, found fashion on their side when they twitted the *Natur-philosophie* with its useless and groundless speculations.

Another propulsive force was even more potent. Between the revolution of July, 1830, and that of February, 1848, a gradual transformation had taken place in republican ideals. The socialistic and communistic tendencies, which the great Revolution had violently repressed, began more and more to dominate the minds of the insurgent reformers in the various states of Europe. Projects of social and economical re-organization on completely new terms were rife, and divided the republican camp between reformers and revolutionists. The various revolutions in 1848, which at first sight had secured the triumph of the more moderate republicans, ultimately in the course of events helped to throw the balance of revolutionary powers into the hands of socialist democracy and more or less pronounced anarchism.

Through the breaches which these movements had made in the bulwarks of the older creeds, the ideas of Schopenhauer, especially after the collapse of the revolutionary successes of 1848, began to find a way. Not that he was an admirer of democracy (socialist or otherwise), or that he took part in the dominant worship of the rising sun of Science. The very contrary is the case. As he had denounced and disowned the feminine supremacy nominally proclaimed in European society, so he waged war against the materialism which the louder champions of Science were proclaiming as the final and most precious result of all her discoveries. If he was contemptuous of the Göttingen professors, Rudolph Wagner and Hermann Lotze, who defended the "Soul," he was not less indignant against the vulgarity of their opponents, Vogt, Büchner, and Moleschott. In his fury against "fellows who have learned nothing but their little bit syringe-ology—no philosophy, no studies in the humanities"—and who yet "in their stupid audacity presume to deal with the nature of things and of the world," he expresses satisfaction at the news that Büchner (on account of his " Force and Matter") had been suspended from his post at Tübingen (1855). Materialism and materialistic science or pseudo-science had evidently no mercy to expect from a Schopenhauerite inquisitor.

With the rising tide of democracy he had little more sympathy. Such sympathy hardly goes with an attitude of mind that holds 300 millions of the vulgar manufactured article called human beings not equal to a single great man, and that finds it sufficient teleological justification of the hard lot of the masses that they supply the necessary surplus out of which science, art, and literature may be cultivated. Still Schopenhauer is not a follower of those happy minds which read evolution as another name for progress, and hail greater complexity of structure as a test of real advance. Man, as he opines, was a dusky-hued inhabitant of warm climates, where he fed on fruits: since then, in the course of extending his abode to colder regions, he has become white and carnivorous. The process, even in these points, Schopenhauer does not count pure improvement. And so too he occasionally adopts the tone of contemporary socialism. The keenest symptom of the world's misery he finds in the fact that six million negro slaves receive daily, on their bare bodies, on an average sixty million lashes, and three million European weavers anxious and hunger-stricken, feebly vegetate in damp houses and cheerless factories. Between serfdom as in Russia, and landlordism as in England, or generally between the serf, the tenant, leaseholder, and hypothecated debtor, the difference is verbal, rather than real. Poverty and slavery are only two forms, one might almost say only two names, of the same thing: and the essence of that thing is that the forces of a labouring man are in major part not applied for his own benefit, but misappropriated to the use of others. He suffers "exploitation": he has to bear a heavier load of labour, and to receive a more stinted satisfaction of his wants, than on a fair average should fall to his share.

But if for a moment the arguments of Engels and Marx carry away his naturally compassionate mind to exaggeration, he is too untrained in the methods of social and political inquiry to carry the problems to deeper issues, and he reverts to his habitual attitude.

It is certain, he admits, that sovereignty belongs to the people. But "Demos" is a sovereign who is always under age, and can never manage his own concerns. Infinite risks assail his unchartered freedom. Whenever released from more legitimate ward, he is the victim of demagogues. Even as a judge, the multitude shows its incapacity: for trial by jury is the worst of all possible modes of criminal procedure, and can only be excused as a relic of the days of barbarism. In governments, monarchy is the only form natural to man: for nature is essentially pledged to the rule of the abler and stronger. Even the animal organism is monarchically constructed, whereof the brain alone is the ruler and driver—a remark, by the way, which has to settle accounts with his contrary estimate of the brain as the "parasite or pensioner of the whole organism," and which throws a beautiful light on the worth of analogical arguments. His real argument, rather, is based on the conviction that so long as the great bulk of mankind is egoistic, unjust, unscrupulous, and mendacious, often malicious and endowed with very scanty intelligence, humanity needs a power, concentrated in one man, standing above the laws, completely irresponsible, making everything bow before it, regarded as a being of higher kind, a ruler by divine grace. The republican system is, on the contrary, as unnatural as it is unfavourable to the arts and sciences and the whole higher life.

These anti-democratic sentiments had received a lively re-enforcement by the events of which Frankfort had been the scene in the revolutionary year 1848. Even in the stormy "March-days" his alarms of social disaster had made him countermand orders he had given for the purchase of books, and for several months he quailed at the prospect of losing all his means in a general *débâcle*. The German parliament which sat at Frankfort had seen gradually emerge in it the antagonism between the more moderate reformers and the thorough-going democrats. The latter party, worsted in parliament, and enraged by the collapse of the war of emancipation in Schleswick-Holstein, threw itself on the support of the mob. Two of the deputies of Austria (against which the indignation was most furious,) Auerswald and Lichnowski, were brutally murdered in the public street—a deed of which even years later Schopenhauer could not speak calmly. On the 18th of September he looked out on the insurgents raising a barricade on the bridge, and heard the shots exchanged between them and the military in an adjoining street. Suddenly loud noises on his door made him proceed to bolt and bar it, under the idea that he was assailed by the "sovereign canaille." He was relieved to hear his maid calling to him that it was a party of Austrian troops, which, having obtained entrance, used his house to shoot from, and even borrowed his opera-glass to help them to detect the enemy. It is, therefore, only what we should expect from an adherent of the party (as it is styled) of law and order, that by the terms of his will, made in 1852, he left the bulk of his estate to be appropriated to the benefit of the soldiers who had been wounded, and the surviving relatives of those who had fallen, at Berlin in 1848, in defence of the royal authority against the socialistic revolution.

Yet though himself unsympathetic with historical criticism, scientific materialism, and democracy, Schopenhauer saw his speculations carried into public favour by the flood which these tendencies contributed to swell. At first it was only a voice here and there in the wilderness which answered his call, but these scattered voices spread the news with zeal around them. To such earliest recruits Schopenhauer, who had the feeling of his vocation of religious teacher, gave the title of apostles and evangelists. The first of them to make himself heard was F. Dorguth, an eccentric "councillor of justice" at Magdeburg, who, in a small tract he published in 1843, conferred on Schopenhauer the title of being the first real systematic thinker in the whole history of literature! This was followed by a succession of similar *brochures* up to Dorguth's death in 1854, at the age of seventy-seven. The old man, who read Schopenhauer with his three daughters, was more loyal than intelligent, and his idol was obliged occasionally to treat what he called the *radotages d'un vieillard* with a half-perplexed indulgence. Yet he had always a kindly word for the "Trumpet" (*Trompete*) as he sportively styled his first apostle. Much more did he owe to the deep "trombone" (*Posaune*) of Julius Frauenstädt, the "arch-evangelist." Frauenstädt, a fluent and active writer, who had skimmed more than one system of thought, first made his master's personal acquaintance in 1847. From that date onwards he continued an assiduous friend and correspondent, working indefatigably by newspaper and magazine article to spread the renown of his chief, assisting him with advice and intervention in the publication of his books, and bringing to his notice every paragraph in which he and his ideas were referred to. Of a long list of works destined more or less to expound Schopenhauer's views to a larger public, may be named "Letters on Schopenhauer's Philosophy," published in 1854. A break, however, occurred in this intimacy. In 1856 Frauenstädt felt himself forced to protest against the injustice with which his words had been misconceived, with the result that for three years the old lion maintained a complete silence, ended however by a letter a few months before his death, written with all the old cordiality.

Adam von Doss, a lawyer in practice at Munich, was, in consideration of a fanatical fervour of discipleship, styled by his master his "Apostle John." He was a silent follower, but his letters were read by Schopenhauer with deep emotion "as a pledge of the action of coming generations." A more public character belongs to the adhesion of E. O. Lindner, assistant editor of the *Vossische Zeitung*, a well-known Liberal newspaper. He made the philosopher's personal acquaintance in the summer of 1852, after reading the "Parerga," and thenceforth was his energetic advocate in the press, while he also popularized his ideas in relation to musical theory. His wife, an Englishwoman, translated from *The Westminster Review*, of April, 1853, Oxenford's article on "Iconoclasm in German Philosophy." After Schopenhauer's death Lindner defended his memory against inadequate representations and personal attacks: particularly as joint author with Frauenstädt of the work "Arthur Schopenhauer: Of him: On him."

The article in question, by John Oxenford—a paper of some twenty pages—though of slight intrinsic importance, claims a passing word of notice as probably the earliest introduction of Schopenhauer to the English public, and as indirectly supplying a stimulus to his popularity in Germany. As its title indicates, Schopenhauer figures in it as the leader of a re-action against the dominant transcendentalism which, under the auspices of Coleridge and others, had been given out in England to be the typical German philosophy. It welcomes in the misanthropic sage of Frankfort an ally in the battle which the English empiricists had been waging against metempirical speculation and theological prejudice. But it is especially for his literary power and skill that Schopenhauer is commended. The larger outlines of his ethical and metaphysical doctrines are stated, with touches of mild regret that his distinguished talents of exposition have not been devoted to the service of more utilitarian and sounder truth. Schopenhauer had written severely of the bigotry of the Church, which degraded what he called "the most intelligent, and in almost every respect the first, nation in Europe;" he had even suggested an anti-clerical mission to England with Strauss in one hand, and Kant's Pure Reason in the other. It was therefore a grateful surprise to him to receive this public recognition from some children of light, even in that benighted land.

Nearer home, besides Dr. Emden, a well-to-do Jewish advocate, who acted as a friendly legal adviser, and whom he lost by death in November, 1858, he had, about 1854, made the acquaintance of W. Gwinner, a young man who was destined to be his biographer, and whom he, with the bequest of his collection of books, appointed his executor. At an earlier date, 1844, began a correspondence with J. A. Becker, a district judge in Alzey, which continued up to Schopenhauer's death. Becker started in his earliest letter some of the more serious difficulties in which the theory of the Will in Schopenhauer is involved, and well deserved the credit which the latter gave him of having of all his disciples most correctly understood him. The correspondence deals with business as well as philosophy, and Becker, who from 1850 onward was settled at Mayence, took frequent opportunities of visiting his friend in the neighbouring Frankfort. The list of these disciples of the first order (from which Emden as a general friend is to be excluded) may be closed by Dr. David Asher, a good English scholar, teacher in a commercial academy at Leipsic, who was attracted by Schopenhauer's theory of music. From 1855 he was an ardent champion and an unwearied correspondent.

Some, though not all of these disciples, who, as may be observed, belonged to the legal and journalistic classes, outside the strictly academic circles, had been drawn to him before the publication of the "Parerga und Paralipomena" (Chips and Scraps) in 1851. This work, which was mainly instrumental in gaining for him the popular ear, had, when finished, been offered to three publishers, who successively declined it. It was only through the mediation of his friend Frauenstädt that Hayn of Berlin undertook to bring it out, paying the author with ten free copies of his own work. Being issued at a lower price than its predecessors, the book (in two volumes), notwithstanding its pedantic title (which the author justified by the allegation that he wrote in the first instance for scholars) attracted by the variety of its contents a fair number of heterogeneous readers. It is a medley, in which each may pick out something to his taste. The longest essays are those on University Philosophy, and on Spiritualistic Phenomena, in Vol. I., and the dialogue on Religion in Vol. II. The last named, savouring of Hume and Voltaire, with a touch of Shelley, is one of those performances which find readers because they give lucid expression to the views which a partly-enlightened public vaguely holds on that ever-interesting topic. Besides these longer essays, there are a series of shorter unsystematic notes, aphoristic and episodic deliverances, on most of the chief problems discussed in his more academic treatises. Several of these are so evidently inspired by personal experience that they have the interest of autobiography. The flavour of personal feeling comes out from every page. Here is no abstract scientific generality, but the self-inspection of a very characteristic individuality, without scruples or limitations to shut the mouth, or even smooth the rudeness of the tongue. Provocative wit, sharp sarcasm, strong feeling, are everywhere—a little cumbrous perhaps, and overcharged with rhetoric, but still wearing that average of decorative style which commends itself to the prevalent, if not to the scholarly, taste. A wide sweep of literary illustration is at the writer's command from all the great authors of ancient and modern times, and is liberally used. Nor is the discussion confined to principles: it descends again and again to instances, even from the humblest. Stories alternate with jests, and the concentrated wisdom of aphorism is a very fair imitation of Chamfort or La Rochefoucauld. It lends itself to quotation, and its sayings are appropriate as well as fine. Metaphysics and physics; natural philosophy, ethics, and politics; the art of life and the laws of literary style; archæology and Sanscrit; ghosts and special providences; language and logic; immortality and asceticism; the reality and the profession of man's life; age and sex;—these are a few of the topics touched on in the " Parerga and Paralipomena."

When *The Westminster Review* had revealed to Germany its yet unrecognized prophet, the " Parerga " found new readers, and threw a reflected popularity on the works which preceded. Schopenhauer saw a second edition of the " Will in Nature " appear in 1854. Five years later he sent out (1859) a third edition of the " World as Will and Idea," and almost his last days in 1860 saw the appearance of a second edition of the " Two Fundamental Problems of Ethics." It is pleasing to see his joy over these signs of success and appreciation, but it is at the same time painful to read in his letters during the period 1847-60 (as published by Frauenstädt and Asher) the eagerness with which he waits to snap up every morsel of applause. A very wolf's hunger for public notice consumes him. His disciples are so many eyes in various corners of the earth to catch the first faintest blush of the coming dawn, and so many messengers to transport to him the news. In this feverish expectancy, every one who fails to recognize his work is judged a malignant; every one who still expounds the old familiar views, or other views than his, is a charlatan and a windbag. To say anything which at all, in tone or tendency, recalls what he has taught, is to be a scoundrelly plagiarist. Nothing can appease or mollify him except complete submission to his dogma—only that submission must put on an air of willing and intelligent acceptance. Even so, it is hard to please him. His two faithful watch-dogs, Frauenstädt and Asher, show a little recalcitrancy when they are expected to impute mean motives to every adversary, and to pour scorn on all who stand aloof. Such an ample treasury of abuse can seldom be found as in the letters to these friends— the terms sometimes so coarse that they have to be faintly veiled in the uncertainty of an initial letter. Probably as a "gentleman" and "man of the world" he feels that a gallant capacity for strong language is a point in which he can hold his own with any mere professor of philosophy.

It is curious—and would be instructive were the data more complete—to note the special attractions to which his different conquests were due. His philosophy, he used to boast, had, like famous Thebes, a hundred gates by which it might be entered. Of some systems of his time it might have been said that strait was the gate, and narrow the way, and few those who found access to their central truth, if truth it were. But within the walls to which led the broad and diverse roads of Schopenhauer's argument, there was gathered a motley, if but a scanty, crowd. One admirer, a brewer, had been specially persuaded by the mystic explanation of sexual love. That is a topic which finds few insensible, and a theory of the universal passion, which explains its vagaries by the wayward necessities of cosmic nature, needs no external recommendation. Many, and among them the philosopher himself, laid stress on the sympathies between his views and the beliefs in animal magnetism and other "spiritualistic" phenomena—if we may antedate a name which came in with the American "rapping" spirits in 1848. Table-turning he holds of supreme importance for his theories, and in his indignation at the scepticism his friends oppose to cases of mediumistic susceptibility, he reminds them there are more things in earth than the dominant philosophies acknowledge. In thus keeping open and guarding that small door leading to the Unseen, Schopenhauer affords a grateful refuge to that love of the mysterious and unearthly, which lingers in many hearts, and refuses to be charmed away by the wisest and wittiest demonstration of the scientific masters that measurable matter is all, and in all. Wherever there lives an unsatisfied soul, longing for direct communication with the potency in universal nature, there is a possible disciple for Schopenhauer. Nor is that all. He who says the Will means the heart—and to place the Will, and not the Intellect, as the most central reality of things—is to secure the suffrages of that numerous body which would prefer that the heart rather than the head should be the supreme motor of the universe. In this identification, with all its ambiguities, lies a strong charm for those with an ineradicable dislike to an abstract rational deity, or to a mere intuitive intelligence. And yet, at the same time, this word Will, shading off into a mere grade of force, does not carry us wholly off the solid material world into a region of mere ideas, and hinders us from assigning the personality of a spiritual being to the "one and all." A slight but sufficient flavour of physical realism clings to the name, and saves it from a too abrupt antagonism to the formulæ of science. And to others still, the dogma of Schopenhauer commended itself as "the religion of the religionless"—a new rock for the faith in the supernatural which had lost all hold on its ancient supports of tradition, and been driven by scientific criticism out of its belief in miracle and legend, yet still craved for something more sustaining than matter and force, and other misty abstractions. For those who can read between the lines, or decipher the palimpsest on which Schopenhauer's doctrines are inscribed, much of the old faith lives disguised in the new; they know that God is not as man, and His thoughts far unlike human; when they hear the attributes and faculties of Will they remember that names are but "sound and smoke, enclouding the blaze of heavenly light," and in the message of pessimism and asceticism they can hear the eternal voice of wisdom, from India to Egypt, from Palestine to Greece, proclaiming vanity of vanities behind and the kingdom of heaven within. Truly, as in hundred-gated Thebes, there is many an access for those who would enter to possess this philosophy.

Schopenhauer, who vaunted that he wrote first and foremost for scholars, was surprised to see that the unlearned were they who came most gladly to hear him, and who made his most zealous evangelists. But this fancy that he belonged to the academic aristocracy, as well as another that he never repeated himself, are only instances to prove how far from rare is self-deception. His strength lies in his one-sidedness, and in the persistency with which he reverts to the same point. Neither his style nor his method are those of the trained scholar, and the public for which he writes is the so-called educated class, possessed of general culture. He is lucid, indeed, or rather, luminous, but it is the lucidity which a forcible intuition, backed up by a wealth of imaginative faculty, seems to shed around it, not the lucidity of a purified and transparent intelligence. Such a pictorial luminosity is more likely to attract the mass of those familiar with the "feel" of ideas, than to persuade the classes who have in some measure penetrated these ideas. As his friend remarked, Schopenhauer's similes afford a clear and striking picture of what he wants you to think, but really contain no solution of the difficulties involved in the thought itself. But for the majority of readers a word which suggests a palpable image, and helps them to picture out in detail what the writer is driving at, is all the demonstration that is held needful.

One need not therefore be astonished, as Schopenhauer was, at the quarter his disciples came from. One day in 1854 he was visited by a lieutenant of the Magdeburg garrison, who was so well grounded in his writings as to be able to cite a passage appropriate to almost any topic —as well he might if he had, as he said, read nothing else for the three years preceding. He brought the news that a score of officers quartered there were equally enthusiastic. Next year another retired officer was among those who laid their epistolary congratulations at his feet. "It is strange," he writes, *àpropos* of this incident, "that my philosophy finds so much acclamation, especially among officers, in Magdeburg, Neisse, Neu-Ruppin, Spandau, and Königsberg. But the whole only in Prussia." After all, it was not so strange that, during these long years of peace, the more intelligent members of the military profession should, in the enforced leisure of garrison life, occasionally show an interest in speculative questions. Even Hegel had in the army those who followed his philosophy: witness the lieutenant of cuirassiers at Pasewalk, who on behalf of himself and other friends there, wrote to ask how he could get a copy of the lectures on the philosophy of religion.

Even from the ladies the old misogynist had at length to welcome what he was pleased to call "a symptom" of intelligence. Half amused he heard of devotees anxiously eliciting on what day of the week their saint was born, in what house, and who was its present possessor. In Dantzic, even, essays were written on his philosophy, and a fervid believer in his gospel had even died with his name on his tongue. Such strange creatures are men! People came to see the lion feed at the *Englischer Hof;* one of these celebrity-hunters would note his distinguished air, another discover a likeness to Talleyrand. On his birthdays copious streams of felicitations began to pour in upon him. Friends at a distance expressed their desire to get some memorial of his countenance. At first a daguerreotype sufficed. In 1855 he accepted the offer of a French painter, Jules Lunteschütz, to take his portrait. The sittings for this purpose were given in what had been the abode of the reputed author of the "Theologia Deutsch," whose mystic piety Schopenhauer found so kindred to his own creed—in the old Deutsches Herrenhaus across the Main, opposite the house (in the *Schöne Aussicht*) where he then lived. The painting was not a success; and Lunteschütz subsequently, by help of a photograph, made out a half-size portrait which gave greater satisfaction. The portrait by this artist, which used to hang in the dining-hall of the *Englischer Hof*, has, in consequence of recent alterations and additions to the building, been relegated to a small reading-room by the entrance. In 1856 he was also painted by Goebel, an artist of Frankfort, and this portrait, like the other, has been multiplied by etchings and lithographs. Lastly, in 1859, his bust was modelled by a young lady artist of Berlin, Elizabeth Ney, who charmed her sitter, and produced a good likeness.

And yet, withal, he was not satisfied. It mattered not that he read in *The Times* that Max Müller, in his essay on the Veda (1853), had said that "Bráhman meant originally force, will, wish, and the propulsive power of creation." The tide did not flow fast enough for his restless wishes. "What a pity," we find him practically saying again and again, "that I don't learn even the half of what is written about me. Don't mind the postage," he adds; "every piece of news about my philosophy is written on my business; and so it is for me to pay the postage." Grandiose dreams that he had caught that world-secret which his predecessors and contemporaries had missed were not likely to be satisfied by anything short of universal assent, and as yet his conquests were in the day of small things, and far from filling a heart that revelled in the idea that, however much the professors of philosophy might profess to see and hear him not, they were really trembling in their hearts at the approach of this new Joshua to their doomed Jericho. So infatuated was he in his self-confidence, that he fell a prey to the imaginative faculty of a poetical youth who, fresh from the enthusiastic meetings of like-minded admirers, confided to him that plans were bruited abroad for establishing at Zürich a chair specially for Schopenhauer's philosophy. And if any such project had been on foot, perhaps Zürich, where more than one German professor found a home in the reactionary times which followed after 1848, would have been the most likely place.

It seemed in 1856 as if the Universities were at last beginning to abandon their supposed policy of ignoring him. The philosophical faculty at Leipsic offered a prize for the best statement and criticism of his system. Alas! the prize-essay, by Rudolph Seydel, treated Schopenhauer as more noteworthy in a literary than a philosophical capacity; and at once the irritable philosopher, convinced that Seydel was the mere tool of a professorial conspiracy, sought to avenge himself by maintaining that another essay, also published in 1857—a laudatory exposition by a son of his Dresden friend Dr. Baehr—was what really deserved the prize. Nothing short of adulation could suffice this hungry heart. Every contemporary fame was bitterness to him —especially that of professors whose god was popularity. Praise of Lotze's "Medical Psychology" he spoke of as laudation of the "old woman's argument," of a "worthless compilation" by "Lotz and Botz"; and when Frauenstädt described Helmholtz and Schopenhauer as (in their theory of vision) "standing on the same ground," the philosopher retorted that it was as bad as saying Montblanc and a mole-hill beside it stood on the same ground.

Except for the almost official friendships of his admirers—touches of the lonely thinker's hand by distant adherents who would fain give their relation the vitality of some personal bond—Schopenhauer was now, as he had long been, a hermit in the city. The throne of philosophy, on which he in imagination sat, was, as thrones generally are, surrounded by a waste. The ceremonial kiss of a fervid disciple cannot make up for the want of the look of true love, and the gratulations of a motley band but poorly satisfy the yearning soul. Most of the friends of his youth had passed the bourne from which no traveller returns. His mother had died in 1838; his sister in 1849; but long before these dates they had passed out of the story of his life. In 1845 he had a visit from Anthime Grégoire de Blésimare, whilom the boy he had played and learned with at Havre, and with whom, up to 1817, he had exchanged letters. At a later date Grégoire, coming across the name of Johanna Schopenhauer on the titlepage of a novel ("Die Tante," published in 1823), had invited his old friend to pay him a visit at his house, Château Juziers, near Meulan, and, that failing, now came with his daughter to Frankfort. But old memories could not be galvanised. Schopenhauer found the

Frenchman in far other planes of thought than his own, and derived little comfort from the meeting. In 1857 he had a short interview with Bunsen, the scholar and ex-diplomatist, who had been for the previous three years settled at Heidelberg. Bunsen excused himself for the too-ready credence he had given to reports of his friend's "Timon-like misanthropy," and they renewed genially recollections of student days at Göttingen.

During his first ten years at Frankfort, Schopenhauer had successively occupied three different lodgings; but in 1843 he settled at No. 17, Schöne Aussicht, on the Main, and there continued till 1859, when he moved into the house next door, No. 16. Alarm about the possibilities of fire had made him prefer the ground-floor. His rooms were simply and usefully furnished, as befitted one who was neither luxurious nor æsthetic, and whose interests lay, not in the fashion or fancies of material decoration, but in the cultivation of a clear intellect and an upright heart. Gutzkow's silly misrepresentations notwithstanding, his was far from a Sybaritic or vulgar style of living. His poodle, of whatever colour it might be, was his only living housemate—and one is glad to know that the faithful dog (no less than other friends and attendants) was duly remembered in his master's will. On his desk stood (after 1851) a plaster-of-Paris bust of Kant—his hero among philosophers—the man whom he owned as his spiritual guide, although, sooth to say, he sometimes seems in captious criticism to make Kant only a pedestal for his own fame. A higher position still was reserved for the bronze Buddha which, after the spring of 1856, stood gilt and glorious on a console in the corner. His devotions to the victoriously-perfect One of the East were not altogether a whim; and if he spoke of the Upanishads in Duperron's translation as his service-book, it meant that his trust was in the Atmân, and his face set towards Nirvana; and indicated that, amidst the ascerbity, vainglory, and egotism his excessive sensitivity led him into, he cherished an inner life in the sanctuary, where he at least craved after the eternal tranquillity of the sage, who, "checking his senses, quiescent, passionless, ready to suffer all things, fixed in ecstasy, sees within himself the Self, sees the universal Soul, the great unborn Self which is undecaying, undying, beyond all fear." The gentle smile on the Buddha's face of glorified renunciation was his consolation against his own yet clinging weaknesses.

Even as others cite the Psalmist's limitation of man's span of life, so he would rely on the Upanishads' assignment of a hundred years. To this pessimist—who held the aims of vulgar imagination, the goal of happiness, so impossible and vain—life for noble ends seemed still worth living. Calmly contented with his infinite realm of thought—with what Jean Paul called "the great ocean of eternity"—he was never smitten by the contagion of that annual epidemic of holiday touring, which he counted a relic of primeval nomadism. His daily run into the suburban by-ways—a practice he kept up in all weathers to his latest years—afforded him the vicissitude he required. For all along he had been accustomed to carry out the old Greek ideal of self-sufficing independence. Even when he longed for recognition, he refused to take any steps to suborn it in his favour. He demanded it as his due, as the reverence which the natural inferior owes to his natural king, as the return of a misguided people from their infatuated worship of mere stage kings to the allegiance due to their true sovereign. It is more because he identifies his pre-eminence with the victory of truth, than for any basely-interested aim, that he challenges their reverence. His is that God-like confidence which cannot understand disobedience, and which explains indifference as wilful high-treason.

He was active to the last. For several months in 1859 he worked three or four hours daily correcting proof-sheets for the third edition of the "World as Will and Idea," and, that finished in November, he gave his best energies to a new edition of his Ethics, which he got off his hands in August, 1860. Well might he say, "How short the day is!" Friends might suggest that hotel life was a strain; he replied, "Mihi est propositum in taberna mori." They might advise change of air; and he quoted "I like my rest; there's no place like home." The final rest was nearer than he supposed. His health for many years, save for petty ailments, had been good; but since April, 1860, he had suffered from palpitation, and was forced at times to stop for rest, as well as to shorten his rapid walks. But it was hard to convince the stout-hearted old man, who had been all his life accustomed to vigorous exercise, that he must bow the head to "the abhorred approaches of old age." His was not the temperament that easily submits to circumstances. In September he had another attack of sudden faintness, followed by inflammation of the lungs, from which, however, he somewhat recovered. He was last seen by his biographer, Dr. Gwinner, on the evening of September 18th. Sitting on his sofa, and complaining that something was amiss with the beating of his heart, he talked cheerfully about literature and politics. As the conversation turned on his writings, he, with a softened accent of his strong voice, expressed his joy that they had in the unbiassed minds of the non-academic world been found a spring of religious peace and comfort. As he spoke in the dim candle-light, it seemed as if some years of service might be reserved for him. But on the 20th he had another bad attack. On the 21st he had risen as usual, and sat down to breakfast. A few minutes after the maid had left, his doctor entered and found him lying back dead in the corner of the sofa, his countenance calm, as if his end had been swift and painless. On the 26th he was interred, with the Evangelical service read at his grave. Over his place of rest lies a flat granite stone, with the sole words " ARTHUR SCHOPENHAUER."

THE END.

INDEX.

A.
Architecture, Schopenhauer's views on, 139-140
Aristotle, quoted, 103
"Arthur Schopenhauer : of him : on him," 196
Asher, Dr. David, 198, 200, 201
Astor, W. B., 67

B.
Becker, J. A., 198
Beneke, F. E., 151
Berlin, 65, 68-73, 147, 149, 155, 163, 165.
Bologna, 142, 143
Bouterwek, Professor, 71
Brockhaus, the publisher, 106-111
Büchner, 191
Bunsen, 67, 209
Byron, Lord, in Italy, 141

C.
Cabanis, influence of, 104-105
Campbell, Thos., 162
Carlyle, Thos., 162

Christianity, Schopenhauer and, 16-18

D.
Dantzic, 22, 24, 29-30, 32-37, 45, 63, 205
Doering, F. W., 57-58
Dorguth, F., 195
Doss, Adam von, 196
Dresden, 73, 85, 89, 96, 147, 154

E.
Eisenach, 147
Emden, Dr., 197, 198

F.
Fernow, K. L., 48, 52
Feuerbach, Anselm von, quoted, 81
Fichte, 16, 64, 65, 69, 70-72, 183, 184; quoted, 117, 129
Florence, 142, 153
Foreign Review and Continental Miscellany, The, 161-162

Frankfort-on-the-Main, 163, 164, 167, 170-179, 185, 193-194, 208-212
Frauenstädt, Dr., 159, 163, 195-196, 198, 200, 201, 208

G.

Gall, the phrenologist, 46
Gastein, 154
Goebel, the artist, 206
Goethe, 48, 49, 56, 75, 83-85, 142, 143
Gotha, 57-58
Göttingen, 64-68, 147
Grégoire, Anthime, 41, 208
Grégoire, Mons., 41
Gwinner, Dr. W., 159, 160, 197-198, 212

H.

Hamburg, 36, 38, 41-42, 46-47, 49, 51, 53
Havre, 41
Haywood, Mr. F., 161-163
Heidelberg, 147
Hegel, 15, 16, 17, 18, 57, 96, 141, 149-150, 163, 183, 184, 189, 205
Helvétius, influence of, 104
Herbart, quoted, 56
Historical method in philosophy, Schopenhauer's view of the, 18-21
Humboldt, W. von, 56

I.

"Iconoclasm in German Philosophy," Oxenford's article on, 196-197
Italy, 138-143, 153

J.

Jagemann, Caroline, 157
Jameson, Dr., 27
Jena, 64, 73

K.

Kant, 16, 64, 66, 75, 109, 116, 117, 161-163, 186, 209; quoted, 23-24
"Karlsbad decrees," 148
Kotzebue, 147

L.

Lancaster, Rev. Mr., 42
"Letter-bag, The," quoted, 110, 153
"Letters on Schopenhauer's Philosophy," Dr. Frauenstädt's, 196
Lichtenstein, Professor, letter to, 148
Lindner, E. O., 196
London, 42
Lotze, Hermann, 191, 207-208
Lunteschütz, Jules, the painter, 205-206
Lyons, 44, 45

M.

Majer, Fr., influence of, 106
Mannheim, 166
Marguet, Caroline L., 152-153, 155
Milan, 143, 153
Moleschott, 191
Müller, Friedrich von, 78
Munich, 153

N.

Naples, 143
Ney, Elizabeth, the artist, 206

O.

Ohra, 63
Oliva, 28-29

"On the Will in Nature," 179-181, 200
"On Vision and Colours," 85-88, 160
Oxenford's article on "Iconoclasm in German Philosophy," 196-197

P.

"Parerga and Paralipomena," 111, 159, 196, 198-200 ; quoted, 80, 106
Paris, 44
Passow, Franz, 58
Philosophy, German and English compared, 11-14
"Philosophical Treatise on the Fourfold Root of the Principle of Sufficient Reason," 11, 73-77
Plato, influence of, 66
Prussia and Dantzic, 32, 34-36

Q.

Quandt, J. G. von, 89

R.

Reinhold, 64
Renan, Mons., quoted, 91
Romanticism, 49-52
Rome, 142
Royal Danish Academy of the Sciences, The, 182-183
Rudolstadt, 73-78

S.

Schaffhausen, 154
Schelling, 16, 64, 65, 183, 184
Schiller, 49, 56, 64
Schlegel, Frederick, his "Language and Wisdom of the Hindoos," 106
Schleiermacher, 68, 69, 70, 150

Schopenhauer, Adele, sister of Arthur, 40, 48, 143, 144, 146, 157, 165, 166, 208
Schopenhauer, Andreas, great-grandfather of Arthur, 24, 30, 31
Schopenhauer, Andreas, grandfather of Arthur, 24
Schopenhauer, Andreas, uncle of Arthur, 25
Schopenhauer, Arthur, more akin to the English than to the German philosopher, 14-15 ; his early training contrasted with that of his predecessors, 15-18 ; his contempt for the historical method in philosophy, 18-20 ; the cause of his success as a teacher, 21 ; born at Dantzic, 22 ; Dutch extraction, 22 ; inherits Dutch mercantile pride, 22-24 ; ancestors, 24-25 ; parents, 25-29 ; birth, 29 ; early years in Dantzic, 30-32 ; removal to Hamburg, 36 ; effects of Dantzic republican training, 36-38 ; his irregular education, 38-39 ; his father's view of a commercial education, 39-40 ; goes to Havre, 41 ; returns to Hamburg, 41 ; school there, 41 ; objects to a commercial life, 41-42 ; but declines the alternative, 42 ; a tour through Europe with his parents, 42-46 ; early traits of character and impressions of his journey, 43-45 ; enters a merchant's office, first at Dantzic, then at Hamburg, 46 ; death of his father, 47 ; his mother becomes an authoress, 47-48 ; he becomes a Romanticist, 49-52 ; dissatisfaction with life, 52 ;

retires from mercantile life, 53; his gratitude to his father, 53-54; school at Gotha and Weimar, 57-58; his regard for the classics, 58-59; his relations with his mother, 59-63; comes into his property, 63; enters the University of Göttingen, 64; his views on Plato and Kant, 66-67; life at Göttingen, 67; meets Wieland, 68; moves to University of Berlin, 68; his contempt for the "university-professor," 69-70; his reported plagiarisms, 70-72; moves to Rudolstadt, 73; takes his Doctor's degree, 73; his "Philosophical Treatise on the Fourfold Root of the Principle of Sufficient Reason," 73-77; returns to Weimar, 78; final rupture with his mother, 78-82; his views on the heredity of the Will and Intellect, 82-83; Goethe seeks Schopenhauer's support of his theories on Light, 83-85; moves to Dresden, 85; essay "On Vision and Colours," 85-88; life at Dresden, 89; his pessimism, 90-91; his contempt for the physical nature of man, 91-93; the nature and growth of his philosophy, 93-99; his view of the true philosopher, 99-100; of genius, 100-104; his reading, 104-106; difficulties with his publisher, 106-108; "The World as Will and Idea," 108-111; Schopenhauer's twofold character, as revealed in his works, 111-112; "The World as Will and Idea" examined, 113-137; visit to Italy, 138-143; bankruptcy of the Dantzic business in which he had a share, 143-147; a college lecturer, 147-150; on his failure, his ill-temper leads him into difficulties, 150-153; visit to Switzerland and Italy, 153-154; his temperament and his relations with women, 155-160; attempts by fresh work, especially translations, to gain popularity, 160-163; moves to Frankfort, 163-164; re-opens correspondence with his mother and sister, 165-166; moves to Mannheim, 166; finally settles at Frankfort, 167; his life at Frankfort, 170-179; "On the Will in Nature," 179-181; gains a prize for an essay on the freedom of the Will, 182; an essay on the basis of morality rejected, 182-183; his fury at rivalry and opposition, 183-185; his two essays published as "The Two Fundamental Problems of Ethics," 185-189; causes of the gradual appreciation of his works, 189-195; the chief of his early disciples, 195-198; "Parerga and Paralipomena," 198-200; his craving for public applause, 200-201; his popularity with the general public, 201-205; portraits of him, 205-206; still dissatisfied with his popularity, 206-207; falls out with the Universities again, 207-208; his mode of life during later years, 208-212; death, 212

Schopenhauer, Heinrich Flor s, father of Arthur, 25-30, 32, 35-36, 39-42, 46, 47, 53, 54

Schopenhauer, Johanna Henriette, mother of Arthur, 26-30, 41, 42, 43, 47-48, 52-53, 59-63, 73, 74, 78-82, 144, 165-166, 181, 208

Schopenhauer, John Frederick, uncle of Arthur, 25

Schulze, G. E., Schopenhauer's teacher at Göttingen, 65, 69

Scientific Society of Drontheim, The, 182

"Senilia," quoted, 110

Seydel, Rudolph, 207

Spinoza, 22

Stuthof, 30-31

Switzerland, 153

T.

Toulon, 45

"Travel-book," 142, 153

Trient, 153, 154

"Two Fundamental Problems of Ethics, The," 185-189, 200, 211

U.

"Upanishads, The," influence of, 105, 210

V.

Venice, 141-143, 153

Vienna, 44, 45

Vogt, 191

W.

Wackenroder, quoted, 97

Wagner, Rudolph, 191

Weimar, 48, 58-59, 60, 64, 73, 78-79, 83, 165

Westminster Review, The, first introduces Schopenhauer to the English public, 195-197, 200

Wieland, 68

Wimbledon, 42-43

Wolf, F. A., 56-57, 69

Wolff, Christian, 15

"World as Will and Idea, The," 108-111, 113-137, 189, 200, 211

BIBLIOGRAPHY.

BY
JOHN P. ANDERSON
(British Museum).

I. WORKS.
II. SELECTIONS.

III. APPENDIX—
Biography, Criticism, etc.
Magazine Articles, etc.

IV. CHRONOLOGICAL
LIST OF WORKS.

I. WORKS.

Arthur Schopenhauer's Sämmtliche Werke. Herausgegeben von J. Frauenstädt. 6 Bde. Leipzig, 1873-4, 8vo.

Arthur Schopenhauer. Von ihm. Ueber ihn. Ein Wort der Vertheidigung von E. O. Lindner und Memorabilien, Briefe und Nachlassstücke von Julius Frauenstädt. Berlin, 1863, 8vo.

Aus Arthur Schopenhauer's handschriftlichem Nachlass. Abhandlungen, Anmerkungen, Aphorismen und Fragmente. Herausgegeben von J. Frauenstädt. Leipzig, 1864, 8vo.

Baltasar Gracian's Hand-Orakel und Kunst der Weltklugheit aus dessen Werken gezogen von Don V. J. de Lastanosa und aus dem Spanischen Original übersetzt von A. Schopenhauer. Nachgelassenes Manuscript. [Edited by J. Frauenstädt.] Leipzig, 1862, 8vo.

Die beiden Grundprobleme der Ethik, behandelt in zwei akademischen Preisschriften. I. Ueber die Freiheit des menschlichen Willens. II. Ueber das Fundament der Moral. Frankfurt-am-Main, 1841, 8vo.

BIBLIOGRAPHY.

Briefwechsel zwischen Arthur Schopenhauer und Johann August Becker. Herausgegeben von J. K. Becker. Leipzig, 1883, 8vo.

Commentatio undecima, exponens Theoriam Colorum Physiologicam, eandemque primariam, auctore Arthurio Schopenhauero Berolinensi. (In Vol. III. pp. 1-58 of "Scriptores Ophthalmologici Minores. Edidit Justus Radius.") Lipsiae, 1830, 8vo.

Parerga und Paralipomena: kleine philosophische Schriften. 2 Bde. Berlin, 1851, 8vo.

—— ——Aphorismen zur Lebensweisheit. Separatausgabe aus "Parerga und Paralipomena." 2 Bdchn. Leipzig, 1886, 8vo.

Schopenhauer Lexikon. Ein philosophisches Wörterbuch, nach Arthur Schopenhauers sämmtliche Schriften, bearbeitet von J. Frauenstädt. 2 Bde. Leipzig, 1871, 8vo.

Select Essays, translated by G. Droppers and C. A. P. Dachsel. Milwaukee, 1881, 8vo.

Ueber das Sehn und die Farben. Leipzig, 1816, 8vo.

——Zweite, verbesserte und vermehrte Auflage. Leipzig, 1854, 8vo.

——Dritte, verbesserte und vermehrte Auflage. Herausgegeben von Julius Frauenstädt. Leipzig, 1870, 8vo.

Ueber den Willen in der Natur. Eine Erörterung der Bestätigungen, welche die Philosophie des Verfassers erhalten hat. Frankfurt-am-Main, 1836, 8vo.

——Zweite, verbesserte und vermehrte Auflage. Frankfurt-am-Main, 1854, 8vo.

——Dritte, verbesserte und vermehrte Auflage, herausgegeben von J. Frauenstädt. Leipzig, 1867, 8vo.

——Vierte Auflage, herausgegeben von J. Frauenstädt. Leipzig, 1878, 8vo.

Ueber die vierfache Wurzel des Satzes vom zureichenden Grunde. Eine philosophische Abhandlung. Rudolstadt, 1813, 8vo.

——Zweite, sehr verbesserte und beträchtlich vermehrte Auflage. Frankfurt-am-Main, 1847, 8vo.

——Dritte, verbesserte und vermehrte Auflage. Herausgegeben von Julius Frauenstädt. Leipzig, 1864, 8vo.

——Vierte Auflage. Herausgegeben von Julius Frauenstädt. Leipzig, 1875, 8vo.

Two Essays by Arthur Schopenhauer. I. On the Fourfold Root of the Principle of Sufficient Reason. II. On the Will in Nature. A literal translation. London, 1889, 8vo. Part of "Bohn's Philosophical Library."

Die Welt als Wille und Vorstellung: vier Bücher, nebst einem Anhange, der die Kritik der Kantischen Philosophie enthält. Leipzig, 1819, 8vo.

——Zweite, durchgängig verbesserte und sehr vermehrte Auflage. 2 Bde. Leipzig, 1844, 8vo.

—— Dritte, verbesserte und beträchtlich vermehrte Auflage. 2 Bde. Leipzig, 1859, 8vo.

——Vierte, vermehrte und verbesserte Auflage. Herausgegeben von Julius Frauenstädt. 2 Bde. Leipzig, 1873, 8vo.

BIBLIOGRAPHY.

——Fünfte Auflage. Herausgegeben von Julius Frauenstädt. 2 Bde. Leipzig, 1879, 8vo.
—— Ueber den Tod und sein Verhältniss zur Unzerstörbarkeit unsers Wesens an sich, etc. Leipzig, 1886, 8vo.
——The World as Will and Idea. Translated from the German by R. B. Haldane, M.A., and J. Kemp, M.A. 3 vols. London, 1883, 8vo.
    Vols. xxii.-xxiv. of "The English and Foreign Philosophical Library."

II. SELECTIONS.

Vom Stillestehen des Verstandes. (Aussprüche für Alle, die redlich forschen wollen.) Bremen, 1868, 8vo.
Arthur Schopenhauer. Lichtstrahlen aus seinen Werken. Mit einer Biographie und Charakteristik Schopenhauer's. Von Julius Frauenstädt. Leipzig, 1862, 8vo.

III. APPENDIX.

BIOGRAPHY, CRITICISM, ETC.

Adler, Helene. — Religion und Moral. Ein Beitrag zur Erziehungsfrage vom Standpunkte der Schopenhauerschen Ethik, etc. Gotha, 1882, 8vo.
Asher, David.—Offenes Sendschreiben an Dr. Arthur Schopenhauer [concerning his philosophical system]. Leipzig, 1855, 8vo.
——Arthur Schopenhauer als Interpret des Göthe'schen Faust, etc. Leipzig, 1859, 8vo.

Asher, David.
——Arthur Schopenhauer. Neues von ihm und über ihn. [Letters, etc.] Berlin, 1871, 8vo.
——Das Endergebniss der Schopenhauer'schen Philosophie in seiner Uebereinstimmung mit einer der ältesten Religionen [*i.e.*, Judaism]. Leipzig, 1885, 8vo.
Bachr, C. G.—Die Schopenhauer'sche Philosophie in ihren Grundzügen dargestellt und kritisch beleuchtet. Dresden, 1857, 8vo.
Bahnsen, Julius F. A.—Zur Philosophie der Geschichte. Eine Kritische Besprechung des Hegel-Hartmann'schen Evolutionismus aus Schopenhauer-'schen Principien. Berlin, 1872, 8vo.
Balche, Alexandre de.—M. Renan et Arthur Schopenhauer. Essai de critique. Odessa, 1870, 8vo.
Bartholmèss, Christian.—Histoire critique des doctrines religieuses de la philosophie moderne. 2 tom. Paris, 1855, 8vo.
    Herbart et Schopenhauer, tom. ii, pp. 423-459.
Barzellotti, Giacomo.—Il pessimismo dello Schopenhauer. Firenze, 1878, 8vo.
Basch, Otto.—Arthur Schopenhauer. [A review of Schopenhauer's philosophy.] Heidelberg, 1877, 8vo.
Bowen, Francis.—Modern Philosophy from Descartes to Schopenhauer and Hartmann. London [1877], 8vo.
    Schopenhauer's Fourfold Root of the Principle of Sufficient Reason, pp. 283-296; Arthur Schopenhauer, pp. 389-428.

Caro, E. M.—Le Pessimisme au XIXᵉ Siècle. Leopardi, Schopenhauer, Hartmann. Paris, 1878, 8vo.

Cohen, Hermann.—Kant's Theorie der Erfahrung. Berlin, 1871, 8vo.
  Schopenhauer's Einwürfe gegen die transcendentale Deduction, pp. 165-182.

Cornill, Adolph.—Arthur Schopenhauer, als Uebergangsformation von einer idealistischen in eine realistiche Weltanschauung dargestellt von A. Cornill. Heidelberg, 1856, 8vo.

Dageraadsman.—Bedankje van een Dageraadsman voor de prise uit de doos van Schopenhauer, aangeboden door A. van der Linde. Amsterdam, 1862, 8vo.

Dorguth, Friedrich. — Schopenhauer in seiner Wahrheit. Mit einem Anhange über das abstrakte Rechte. Magdeburg, 1845, 8vo.

——Das Licht der wahrhaften kosmischen dem Irrlichte der Hegel'schen Dialektik gegenüber. Ein Schreiben an den Herrn Dr. Arthur Schopenhauer. Magdeburg, 1584, 8vo.

——Vermischte Bemerkungen über die Philosophie Schopenhauer's, ein Brief an den Meister. Magdeburg, 1852, 8vo.

Dühring, E. — Kritische Geschichte der Philosophie, etc. Berlin, 1869, 8vo.
  Schopenhauer und sein Pessimismus, pp. 446-479.

Du Mont, Emerich.—Der Fortschritt im Lichte der Lehren Schopenhauer's und Darwin's. Leipzig, 1876, 8vo.

Eiser, Otto.—Andeutungen über Wagner's Beziehung zu Schopenhauer, etc. Chemnitz, 1878, 8vo.

Erdmann, Johann E.—Versuch einer wissenschaftlichen Darstellung der Geschichte der neuern Philosophie. 3 Bde. Riga, 1834-53, 8vo.
  Schopenhauer, Bd. iii., pp. 381-412; Schlussbemerkung zu Herbart und Schopenhauer, pp. 412-417.

Feuchtersleben, Ernest von.—Zur Diätetik der Seele. Mit Begleitstellen aus den Werken von Schopenhauer, etc. Hamburg, 1880, 8vo.

Fichte, Imanuel H.—System der Ethik. Leipzig, 1850, 8vo.
  Arthur Schopenhauer, Th. i., pp. 394-415.

Fortlage, C. — Genetische Geschichte der Philosophie seit Kant. Leipzig, 1852, 8vo.
  Schopenhauer, pp. 407-423.

Foucher de Careil, Alexandre.—Hegel et Schopenhauer: études sur la philosophie allemande moderne depuis Kant jusqu'à nos jours. Paris, 1862, 8vo.

——Another edition. Aus dem Französischen übersetzt von J. Singer. Wien, 1888, 8vo.

Frauenstädt, Julius.—Briefe über die Schopenhauer'sche Philosophie. Leipzig, 1854, 8vo.

——Neue Briefe über die Schopenhauer'sche Philosophie. Leipzig, 1876 [1875], 8vo.

Frommann, Hermann. — Arthur Schopenhauer. Drei Vorlesungen. Jena, 1872, 8vo.

Frugifer, *pseud*.—Die Hoffnungen der deutschen Schauspielkunst, gegründet auf die Principien der Schopenhauer'schen Philosophie. Oldenburg, 1864, 8vo.

Galletti, Baldassare. — Noto di critica odierno con appendice l'Amore, la donne, ed il matrimonio di A. Schopenhauer. Palermo, 1881, 4to.

Gizycki, Georg von. — Kant und Schopenhauer. Zwei Aufsätze. Leipzig, 1899, 8vo.

Grisebach, Eduard. — Edita und Inedita Schoperhaueriana. Eine Schopenhauer - Bibliographie, etc. Leipzig, 1888, 4to.

Guetzlaff, Victor. — Schopenhauer ueber die Thiere und den Thierschutz, etc. Berlin, 1879, 8vo.

Gwinner, Wilhelm. — Arthur Schopenhauer aus persönlichen Umgange dargestellt. Ein Blick auf sein Leben, seinen Charakter und seine Lehre. Leipzig, 1862, 8vo.

——Schopenhauer's Leben. Zweite, umgearbeitete und vermehrte Auflage der Schrift: Arthur Schopenhauer aus persönlichen Umgange dargestellt, etc. Leipzig, 1878, 8vo.

——Schopenhauer und seine Freunde, etc. Leipzig, 1863, 8vo.

——Denkrede auf Arthur Schopenhauer, etc. Leipzig, 1888, 8vo.

Harms, Friedrich. — Arthur Schopenhauer's Philosophie. Ein Vorträge, etc. Berlin, 1874, 8vo.

Hartmann, Carl Robert E. von. — Schelling's positive Philosophie als Einheit von Hegel und Schopenhauer. Berlin, 1869, 8vo.

——Neukantianismus, Schopenhauerianismus, und Hegelianismus in ihrer Stellung zu den philosophischen Aufgaben der Gegenwart. Berlin, 1877, 8vo.

Hartmann, Carl Robert E. von. ——Gesammelte Studien und Aufsätze. Berlin, 1876, 8vo.
Schopenhauer und die Farbenlehre, pp. 520-525; Schopenhauer's Panthelismus, pp. 636-649.

——Philosophische Fragen der Gegenwart. Leipzig, 1885, 8vo.
Mein Verhältniss zu Schopenhauer, pp. 25-37; Die Schopenhauer'sche Schule, pp. 38-57.

——Kritische Wanderungen durch die Philosophie der Gegenwart. Leipzig, 1890, 8vo.
Zu Schopenhauer's hundertjährigem Geburtstag, pp. 26-42.

Hausegger, Friedrich von. — Richard Wagner und Schopenhauer. Eine Darlegung der philosophischen Anschauungen Richard Wagner's an der Hand seiner Werke. Leipzig, 1878, 8vo.

Haym, R. — Arthur Schopenhauer. Berlin, 1864, 8vo.

Hermann, Ernst. — Woher und Wohin? Schopenhauer's Antwort auf die letzten Lebensfragen, zusammengefasst und ergänzt von E. Hermann. Bonn, 1877, 8vo.

Hoffmann, Franz. — Philosophische Schriften. 8 Bd. Erlangen, 1868-1882, 8vo.
Arthur Schopenhauer aus persönlichem Umgange dargestellt von Gwinner, Bd. ii., pp. 190-196; Aus Arthur Schopenhauer's handschriftlichem Nachlass, von J. Frauenstädt, Bd. iv., pp. 121-147; Arthur Schopenhauer, von R. Haym, Bd. iv., pp. 147-155; Der Pessimismus und die Ethik Schopenhauer's von Kiy, Bd. iv., pp. 156-159; Arthur Schopenhauer und Franz Baader, Bd. vi., pp. 371-387; Arthur Schopenhauer, Bd. viii., pp. 267-319.

Janssen, Johannes. — Zeit und Lebensbilder. Freiburg im Breisgau, 1876, 8vo.
Der Philosoph Arthur Schopenhauer, pp. 83-104.

Jellinek, Georg. — Die Weltanschauungen Leibnitz'und Schopenhauer's, ihre Gründe und ihre Berechtigung, etc. Wien, 1872, 8vo.

Kiy, Victor. — Der Pessimismus und die Ethik Schopenhauer's. Berlin, 1866, 8vo.

Klee, Hermann. — Grundzüge einer Aesthetik nach Schopenhauer. Berlin, 1875, 8vo.

Klencke, P. F. Hermann. — Vom phantastischen Pessimismus zum freudigen Realismus: Schopenhauer und Spinoza. 2 pts. Leipzig [1882], 8vo.

Klotschke, Hermann. — Charakterzuge aus dem Leben Arthur Schopenhauer. Zeitz, 1881, 8vo.

Kober, Carl R. — Das Mitleid als die moralische Triebfeder. Ein Beitrag, zur Kritik der Schopenhauer'schen Ethik, etc. Leipzig [1884], 8vo.

Koeber, Raphael. — Schopenhauer's Erlösungslehre, etc. Berlin, 1881, 8vo.

—— Die Philosophie A. Schopenhauers. Leipzig, 1888, 8vo.

Korten, H. L. — Quomodo Schopenhauer ethicam fundamento metaphysico constituere conatus sit. Dissertatio, etc. Halis Saxonum [1864], 8vo.

Kroenig, A. — Das Dasein Gottes und das Glück der Menschen. Materialisticherfahrungs philosophische Studien ... über die Hauptlehren Kant's und Schopenhauer's. Berlin, 1874, 8vo.

Laban, Ferdinand. — Die Schopenhauer-Literatur. Versuch einer Chronologischen Uebersicht derselben. Leipzig, 1880, 8vo.

Last, E. — Mehr Licht! Die Hauptsätze Kant's und Schopenhauer's in allgemein verständlicher Darlegung. Leipzig, 1880, 8vo.

Lehmann, Otto. — Ueber Kant's Principien der Ethik und Schopenhauer's Beurteilung derselben. Eine kritische Studie. Berlin, 1880, 8vo.

Liebmann, Otto. — Kant und die Epigonen, etc. Stuttgart, 1865, 8vo.
Die transcendente Richtung-Schopenhauer, pp. 157-203.

—— Ueber den individuellen Beweis für die Freiheit des Willens. Stuttgart, 1866, 8vo.
Kritik der Schopenhauerschen Freiheitslehre, pp. 65-101.

Mayer, Gottlob. — Heraklit von Ephesus und Arthur Schopenhauer. Eine historisch-philosophisch Parallele. Heidelberg, 1886, 8vo.

Meltzl von Lomnitz, Hugo. — Schopenhauer A. bölcselmi elödei. Kolozsvár, 1873, 8vo.

—— Denkmünze zum Centenarium Schopenhauers, etc. Leipzig, 1886, 8vo.

Meyer, Juergen B. — Weltelend und Weltschmerz. Eine Rede gegen Schopenhauer's und Hartmann's Pessimismus. Bonn 1872, 8vo.

—— Arthur Schopenhauer als Mensch und Denker. Berlin, 1872, 8vo.
Pt. 145, ser. vii. of "Sammlung gemeinverständlicher wissenschaftlicher Vorträge, herausgegeben von Virchow und Holtzendorff."

Mueller, Moritz. — Über "der Weisheit letzten Schluss." Mit kritischen Bemerkungen über pessimistische Ansichten und Aussprüche von A. Schopenhauer, etc. Berlin, 1886, 8vo.

Nagel, Wilhelm. — Begleitende Bemerkungen zu Schopenhauers philosophischen Systeme "die Welt als Wille und Vorstellung." Bremen, 1861, 8vo.

Nietzsche, Friedrich.—Unzeitgemässe Betrachtungen. Drittes Stuck: Schopenhauer als Erzieher. Schloss-Chemnitz, 1874, 8vo.

Nolen, Désiré.—La Critique de Kant, etc. Paris, 1875, 8vo.
Schopenhauer, pp. 441-443.

Paoli, Alessandro.—Lo Schopenhauer e il Rosmini. Roma, 1878, 8vo.

Pawlicki, S. Z.—De Schopenhaueri doctrina et Philosophandi ratione. Dissertatio philosophica. Vratislaviæ [1865], 8vo.

Peters, Carl.—Arthur Schopenhauer als Philosoph und Schriftsteller. Eine Skizze. Berlin, 1880, 8vo.

Reich, Emil.—Schopenhauer als Philosoph der Tragödie. Eine kritische Studie. Wien, 1888, 8vo.

Ribot, Théodule.—La Philosophie de Schopenhauer. Paris, 1885, 18mo.

Rosenkranz, K. — Hegel als deutscher Nationalphilosoph. Leipzig, 1870, 8vo.
Schopenhauer, pp. 269-276.

Rousseau, J. J.—Parallelen. J. J. Rousseau, Schopenhauer, Grillparzer, etc. Eine Studie. Wien, 1875, 8vo.

Sanctis, Francesco de. Saggi Critici. Napoli, 1869, 8vo.
Schopenhauer e Leopardi, pp. 238-291.

Sauerlaender, Ernst. — Goethe's Faust und die Schopenhauer'sche Philosophie. Frankfurt-am-Main, 1865, 8vo.

Scheffer, Wessel.—Arthur Schopenhauer. De Philosophie van het Pessimisme. Leiden, 1870, 8vo.

Schopenhauer, Arthur. — Wegweiser zur Philosophie Arthur Schopenhauer's. Chemnitz, 1879, 8vo.

Schwegler, Friedrich Carl Albert. —A History of Philosophy, translated by J. H. Seelye. New York, 1881, 8vo.
Schopenhauer, pp. 427-442.

Seidlitz, Carl von.—Dr. Arthur Schopenhauer vom medicinischen Standpuncte aus betrachtet. Dorpat, 1872, 8vo.

Seydel, Rudolf.—Schopenhauer's Philosophisches System dargestellt und beurtheilt. Leipzig, 1857, 8vo.

Siebentist, August. — Schopenhauer's Philosophie der Tragödie. Pressburg, 1880, 8vo.

Spiegel, G. von.—L'Esprit de la Philosophie de Schopenhauer. Darmstadt, 1863, 8vo.

Stern, J.—Arthur Schopenhauer. Zu dessen hundertjährigen Geburtstag. [An account of his life and doctrines.] Zürich, 1888, 8vo.

Stieglitz, Theodor. — Grundsätze der historischen Entwicklung aus den übereinstimmenden Principien der Philosophie Arthur Schopenhauer's, etc. Wien, 1881, 8vo.

Suhle, Berthold.—Arthur Schopenhauer und die Philosophie der Gegenwart, etc. Bd. 1. Berlin, 1862, 8vo.
No more published.

Sully, James. — Pessimism, a

history and a criticism. London, 1877, 8vo.
   Schopenhauer, pp. 74-105, etc.

Thilo, C. A.—Über Schopenhauer's ethischen Atheismus. Leipzig, 1868, 8vo.

Tschofen, Johann M.—Die Philosophie Arthur Schopenhauers in ihrer Relation zur Ethik. München, 1879, 8vo.

Tsertelev, Prince D.—Filosofiya Shopengauera Pervaya Chast. Theoriya poznaniya i metafizika. St. Petersburg, 1880, 8vo.

Ueberweg, Friedrich.—Grundriss der Geschichte der Philosophie, etc. 3 Thle. Berlin, 1863, 8vo.
   Schopenhauer, Th. iii., pp. 264-275.

——— History of Philosophy. Translated by G. S. Morris. London, 1874, 8vo.
   Schopenhauer, vol. ii., pp. 255-264.

Vadalà-Papale G. — La dottrina filosofico giuridica di Schopenhauer e di Hartmann. Studio critico - sistematico. Trani [1889], 8vo.

Venetianer, Moritz. — Schopenhauer als Scholastiker. Eine Kritik der Schopenhauer'schen Philosophie, etc. Berlin, 1873, 8vo.

Wagner, Wilhelm Richard.—Beethoven. With a supplement from the Philosophical Works of Arthur Schopenhauer. Translated by E. Dannreuther. London 1880, 8vo.

Wallace, Professor W. — The Article "Arthur Schopenhauer." (*Encyclopædia Britannica*, vol. xxi., pp. 448-458.) London, 1886, 4to.

Willy, Rudolf.—Schopenhauer in seinem Verhältniss zu J. G. Fichte und Schelling. Zürich, 1883, 8vo.

Wollny, F.—Ueber Freiheit und Charakter des Menschen. Leipzig, 1876, 8vo.
   Kritik der Schopenhauer'schen Theorie von der Unveränderlichkeit des Charakters, pp. 47-52.

Wurzbach, Alfred von.—Arthur Schopenhauer. Wien, 1871, 12mo.
   Heft vi. of "Zeitgenossen. Biographische Skizzen von A. von Wurzbach."

Wyncken, Ernst Friedrich.—Das Naturgesetz der Seele, oder Herbart und Schopenhauer, eine Synthese. Hannover, 1869, 8vo.

Zange, E. M. F.—Ueber das Fundament der Ethik. Eine kritische Untersuchung über Kant's und Schopenhauer's Moralprinzip. Leipzig, 1872, 8vo.

Zimmern, Helen.—Arthur Schopenhauer, his life and his philosophy. London, 1876, 8vo.

MAGAZINE ARTICLES, ETC.

Schopenhauer, Arthur.—Contemporary Review, by H. Lawrenny, vol. 21, 1873, pp. 440-463.—Fortnightly Review, by F. Hueffer, vol. 20 N.S., 1876, pp. 773-792. — Christian Examiner, by F. H. Hedge, vol. 76, 1864, pp. 46-60.—Theological Review, by H. S. Solly, vol. 13, 1876, pp. 395-412.—Illustrirte Zeitung, 4 Dec., 1858.—Europa, No. 5, 1862, pp. 128-136.—Saturday Review, vol. 53, 1882, pp. 556, 557.—Dial, by W. M. Payne, vol. 4, 1884, pp. 245-248, 320.

Schopenhauer, Arthur.

——*A Buddhist Contemporary in Germany.* Revue des Deux Mondes, by P. Challemel-Lacour, tom. 86, 1870, pp. 296-332.

—— *and French Physiology.* Revue des Deux Mondes, by Paul Janet, tom. 39, 1880, pp. 35-59.

——*and Herbart.* Zeitschrift für Philosophie, by J. L. Erdmann, Bd. 21, 1852, pp. 209-226.

——*and his Pessimism.* Methodist Quarterly, by J. P. Lacroix, vol. 58, 1876, pp. 487-510.

——*and Kant.* Journal of Speculative Philosophy, by J. H. Stirling, vol. 13, 1879, pp. 1-50; and by Professor Caird, vol. 13, pp. 215-220.

——*and von Hartmann.* Journal of Speculative Philosophy, by W. R. Morse, vol. 11, 1877, pp. 152-160.

——*in English.* Nation, by H. T. Finck, vol. 42, 1886, pp. 510, 511.

——*Literary Aspects of Work of.* New Quarterly Magazine, by Francis Hueffer, vol. 8, 1877, pp. 352-378.

——*on Men, Books, and Music.* Fraser's Magazine, by M. B. Edwards, vol. 19 N.S., 1879, pp. 769-777; same article, Appleton's Journal, vol. 7 N.S., pp. 162-168.

——*Pessimism of, and German Thought.* Princeton Review, by A. Alexander, March 1878, pp. 492-504.

——*Philosophy of.* Westminster Review, by John Oxenford, vol. 3 N.S., 1853, pp. 388-407.—North American Review, by E. Gryzanovski, vol. 117, 1873, pp. 37-80.—International Review, by C. F. Thwing, vol. 4, 1877, pp. 823-837.—Presbyterian Quarterly, vol. 5, 1876, pp. 93-117.—Mind, by R. Adamson, vol. 1, 1876, pp. 491-509.—Journal of Speculative Philosophy, by F. Harms, vol. 9, 1875, pp. 113-138.—Journal des Savants, by Ch. Lévêque, 1874, pp. 782-796. — Revue Germanique, by C. Dollfus, tom. 8, pp. 367-394.

——*Views of Life.* Cornhill Magazine, vol. 33, 1876, pp. 433-443.

——*World as Will and Idea.* Critic, vol. 4, 1884, pp. 50, 51.—Literary World (Boston), vol. 15, 1884, pp. 210, 211.—Hermes, No. 7, 1820, pp. 131-149.

IV. CHRONOLOGICAL LIST OF WORKS.

Ueber die vierfache Wurzel des Satzes vom zureichenden Grunde . . 1813
Ueber des Sehen und die Farben 1816
Die Welt als Wille und Vorstellung . . . 1819
Theoria colorum physiologica, eademque primaria 1830
(In *Scriptores opthalmologici minores, ed. Justus Radius.*)
Ueber den Willen in der Natur 1836
Die beiden Grundprobleme der Ethik . . . 1841
Parerga und Paralipomena 1851

Baltasar Gracian's Hand-Orakel und Kunst der Weltklugheit, etc. (*Translated.*) . . 1862
Aus A. Schopenhauer's handschriftlichem Nachlass 1864
Briefwechsel zwischen A. Schopenhauer und J. A. Becker 1883

Printed by WALTER SCOTT, *Felling, Newcastle-on-Tyne.*

THE SCOTT LIBRARY.

Cloth, Uncut Edges, Gilt Top.   Price 1s. 6d. per Volume.

VOLUMES ALREADY ISSUED—

1. MALORY'S ROMANCE OF KING ARTHUR AND THE Quest of the Holy Grail. Edited by Ernest Rhys.

2. THOREAU'S WALDEN. WITH INTRODUCTORY NOTE by Will H. Dircks.

3. THOREAU'S "WEEK." WITH PREFATORY NOTE BY Will H. Dircks.

4. THOREAU'S ESSAYS. EDITED, WITH AN INTROduction, by Will H. Dircks.

5. CONFESSIONS OF AN ENGLISH OPIUM-EATER, ETC. By Thomas De Quincey. With Introductory Note by William Sharp.

6. LANDOR'S IMAGINARY CONVERSATIONS. SELECTED, with Introduction, by Havelock Ellis.

7. PLUTARCH'S LIVES (LANGHORNE). WITH INTROductory Note by B. J. Snell, M.A.

8. BROWNE'S RELIGIO MEDICI, ETC. WITH INTROduction by J. Addington Symonds.

9. SHELLEY'S ESSAYS AND LETTERS. EDITED, WITH Introductory Note, by Ernest Rhys.

10. SWIFT'S PROSE WRITINGS. CHOSEN AND ARRANGED, with Introduction, by Walter Lewin.

11. MY STUDY WINDOWS. BY JAMES RUSSELL LOWELL. With Introduction by R. Garnett, LL.D.

12. LOWELL'S ESSAYS ON THE ENGLISH POETS. WITH a new Introduction by Mr. Lowell.

13. THE BIGLOW PAPERS. BY JAMES RUSSELL LOWELL. With a Prefatory Note by Ernest Rhys.

London: WALTER SCOTT, LIMITED, 24 Warwick Lane.

THE SCOTT LIBRARY—continued.

14 GREAT ENGLISH PAINTERS. SELECTED FROM Cunningham's *Lives*. Edited by William Sharp.

15 BYRON'S LETTERS AND JOURNALS. SELECTED, with Introduction, by Mathilde Blind.

16 LEIGH HUNT'S ESSAYS. WITH INTRODUCTION AND Notes by Arthur Symons.

17 LONGFELLOW'S "HYPERION," "KAVANAH," AND "The Trouveres." With Introduction by W. Tirebuck.

18 GREAT MUSICAL COMPOSERS. BY G. F. FERRIS. Edited, with Introduction, by Mrs. William Sharp.

19 THE MEDITATIONS OF MARCUS AURELIUS. EDITED by Alice Zimmern.

20 THE TEACHING OF EPICTETUS. TRANSLATED FROM the Greek, with Introduction and Notes, by T. W. Rolleston.

21 SELECTIONS FROM SENECA. WITH INTRODUCTION by Walter Clode.

22 SPECIMEN DAYS IN AMERICA. BY WALT WHITMAN. Revised by the Author, with fresh Preface.

23 DEMOCRATIC VISTAS, AND OTHER PAPERS. BY Walt Whitman. (Published by arrangement with the Author.)

24 WHITE'S NATURAL HISTORY OF SELBORNE. WITH a Preface by Richard Jefferies.

25 DEFOE'S CAPTAIN SINGLETON. EDITED, WITH Introduction, by H. Halliday Sparling.

26 MAZZINI'S ESSAYS: LITERARY, POLITICAL, AND Religious. With Introduction by William Clarke.

27 PROSE WRITINGS OF HEINE. WITH INTRODUCTION by Havelock Ellis.

28 REYNOLDS'S DISCOURSES. WITH INTRODUCTION by Helen Zimmern.

29 PAPERS OF STEELE AND ADDISON. EDITED BY Walter Lewin.

30 BURNS'S LETTERS. SELECTED AND ARRANGED with Introduction, by J. Logie Robertson, M.A.

London: WALTER SCOTT, LIMITED, 24 Warwick Lane.

THE SCOTT LIBRARY—continued.

31 VOLSUNGA SAGA. WILLIAM MORRIS. WITH INTROduction by H. H. Sparling.

32 SARTOR RESARTUS. BY THOMAS CARLYLE. WITH Introduction by Ernest Rhys.

33 SELECT WRITINGS OF EMERSON. WITH INTROduction by Percival Chubb.

34 AUTOBIOGRAPHY OF LORD HERBERT. EDITED, with an Introduction, by Will H. Dircks.

35 ENGLISH PROSE, FROM MAUNDEVILLE TO Thackeray. Chosen and Edited by Arthur Galton.

36 THE PILLARS OF SOCIETY, AND OTHER PLAYS. BY Henrik Ibsen. Edited, with an Introduction, by Havelock Ellis.

37 IRISH FAIRY AND FOLK TALES. EDITED AND Selected by W. B. Yeats.

38 ESSAYS OF DR. JOHNSON, WITH BIOGRAPHICAL Introduction and Notes by Stuart J. Reid.

39 ESSAYS OF WILLIAM HAZLITT. SELECTED AND Edited, with Introduction and Notes, by Frank Carr.

40 LANDOR'S PENTAMERON, AND OTHER IMAGINARY Conversations. Edited, with a Preface, by H. Ellis.

41 POE'S TALES AND ESSAYS. EDITED, WITH INTROduction, by Ernest Rhys.

42 VICAR OF WAKEFIELD. BY OLIVER GOLDSMITH. Edited, with Preface, by Ernest Rhys.

43 POLITICAL ORATIONS, FROM WENTWORTH TO Macaulay. Edited, with Introduction, by William Clarke.

44 THE AUTOCRAT OF THE BREAKFAST-TABLE. BY Oliver Wendell Holmes.

45 THE POET AT THE BREAKFAST-TABLE. BY OLIVER Wendell Holmes.

46 THE PROFESSOR AT THE BREAKFAST-TABLE. BY Oliver Wendell Holmes.

47 LORD CHESTERFIELD'S LETTERS TO HIS SON. Selected, with Introduction, by Charles Sayle.

London: WALTER SCOTT, LIMITED, 24 Warwick Lane.

THE SCOTT LIBRARY —continued.

48 STORIES FROM CARLETON. SELECTED, WITH INTROduction, by W. Yeats.

49 JANE EYRE. BY CHARLOTTE BRONTË. EDITED BY Clement K. Shorter.

50 ELIZABETHAN ENGLAND. EDITED BY LOTHROP Withington, with a Preface by Dr. Furnivall.

51 THE PROSE WRITINGS OF THOMAS DAVIS. EDITED by T. W. Rolleston.

52 SPENCE'S ANECDOTES. A SELECTION. EDITED, with an Introduction and Notes, by John Underhill.

53 MORE'S UTOPIA, AND LIFE OF EDWARD V. EDITED, with an Introduction, by Maurice Adams.

54 SADI'S GULISTAN, OR FLOWER GARDEN. TRANSlated, with an Essay, by James Ross.

55 ENGLISH FAIRY AND FOLK TALES. EDITED BY E. Sidney Hartland.

56 NORTHERN STUDIES. BY EDMUND GOSSE. WITH a Note by Ernest Rhys.

57 EARLY REVIEWS OF GREAT WRITERS. EDITED BY E. Stevenson.

58 ARISTOTLE'S ETHICS. WITH GEORGE HENRY Lewes's Essay on Aristotle prefixed.

59 LANDOR'S PERICLES AND ASPASIA. EDITED, WITH an Introduction, by Havelock Ellis.

60 ANNALS OF TACITUS. THOMAS GORDON'S TRANSlation. Edited, with an Introduction, by Arthur Galton.

61 ESSAYS OF ELIA. BY CHARLES LAMB. EDITED, with an Introduction, by Ernest Rhys.

62 BALZAC'S SHORTER STORIES. TRANSLATED BY William Wilson and the Count Stenbock.

63 COMEDIES OF DE MUSSET. EDITED, WITH AN Introductory Note, by S. L. Gwynn.

64 CORAL REEFS. BY CHARLES DARWIN. EDITED, with an Introduction, by Dr. J. W. Williams.

London: WALTER SCOTT, LIMITED, 24 Warwick Lane.

THE SCOTT LIBRARY—continued.

65 SHERIDAN'S PLAYS. EDITED, WITH AN INTROduction, by Rudolf Dircks.

66 OUR VILLAGE. BY MISS MITFORD. EDITED, WITH an Introduction, by Ernest Rhys.

67 MASTER HUMPHREY'S CLOCK, AND OTHER STORIES. By Charles Dickens. With Introduction by Frank T. Marzials.

68 TALES FROM WONDERLAND. BY RUDOLPH Baumbach. Translated by Helen B. Dole.

69 ESSAYS AND PAPERS BY DOUGLAS JERROLD. EDITED by Walter Jerrold.

70 VINDICATION OF THE RIGHTS OF WOMAN. BY Mary Wollstonecraft. Introduction by Mrs. E. Robins Pennell.

71 "THE ATHENIAN ORACLE." A SELECTION. EDITED by John Underhill, with Prefatory Note by Walter Besant.

72 ESSAYS OF SAINT-BEUVE. TRANSLATED AND Edited, with an Introduction, by Elizabeth Lee.

73 SELECTIONS FROM PLATO. FROM THE TRANSlation of Sydenham and Taylor. Edited by T. W. Rolleston.

74 HEINE'S ITALIAN TRAVEL SKETCHES, ETC. Translated by Elizabeth A. Sharp. With an Introduction from the French of Theophile Gautier.

75 SCHILLER'S MAID OF ORLEANS. TRANSLATED, with an Introduction, by Major-General Patrick Maxwell.

76 SELECTIONS FROM SYDNEY SMITH. EDITED, WITH an Introduction, by Ernest Rhys.

77 THE NEW SPIRIT. BY HAVELOCK ELLIS.

78 THE BOOK OF MARVELLOUS ADVENTURES. FROM the "Morte d'Arthur." Edited by Ernest Rhys. [This, together with No. 1, forms the complete "Morte d'Arthur."]

79 ESSAYS AND APHORISMS. BY SIR ARTHUR HELPS. With an Introduction by E. A. Helps.

80 ESSAYS OF MONTAIGNE. SELECTED, WITH A Prefatory Note, by Percival Chubb.

81 THE LUCK OF BARRY LYNDON. BY W. M. Thackeray. Edited by F. T. Marzials.

London: WALTER SCOTT, LIMITED, 24 Warwick Lane.

THE SCOTT LIBRARY—continued.

82 SCHILLER'S WILLIAM TELL. TRANSLATED, WITH an Introduction, by Major-General Patrick Maxwell.

83 CARLYLE'S ESSAYS ON GERMAN LITERATURE. With an Introduction by Ernest Rhys.

84 PLAYS AND DRAMATIC ESSAYS OF CHARLES LAMB. Edited, with an Introduction, by Rudolf Dircks.

85 THE PROSE OF WORDSWORTH. SELECTED AND Edited, with an Introduction, by Professor William Knight.

86 ESSAYS, DIALOGUES, AND THOUGHTS OF COUNT Giacomo Leopardi. Translated, with an Introduction and Notes, by Major-General Patrick Maxwell.

87 THE INSPECTOR-GENERAL A RUSSIAN COMEDY. By Nikolai V. Gogol. Translated from the original, with an Introduction and Notes, by Arthur A. Sykes.

88 ESSAYS AND APOTHEGMS OF FRANCIS, LORD BACON: Edited, with an Introduction, by John Buchan.

89 PROSE OF MILTON: SELECTED AND EDITED, WITH an Introduction, by Richard Garnett, LL.D.

London: WALTER SCOTT, LIMITED, 24 Warwick Lane.

GREAT WRITERS.

A NEW SERIES OF CRITICAL BIOGRAPHIES.

Edited by ERIC ROBERTSON and FRANK T. MARZIALS.

A Complete Bibliography to each Volume, by J. P. ANDERSON, British Museum, London.

Cloth, Uncut Edges, Gilt Top. Price 1/6.

VOLUMES ALREADY ISSUED—

LIFE OF LONGFELLOW. By PROF. ERIC S. ROBERTSON.
"A most readable little work."—*Liverpool Mercury.*

LIFE OF COLERIDGE. By HALL CAINE.
"Brief and vigorous, written throughout with spirit and great literary skill."—*Scotsman.*

LIFE OF DICKENS. By FRANK T. MARZIALS.
"Notwithstanding the mass of matter that has been printed relating to Dickens and his works ... we should, until we came across this volume, have been at a loss to recommend any popular life of England's most popular novelist as being really satisfactory. The difficulty is removed by Mr. Marzials's little book."—*Athenæum.*

LIFE OF DANTE GABRIEL ROSSETTI. By J. KNIGHT.
"Mr. Knight's picture of the great poet and painter is the fullest and best yet presented to the public."—*The Graphic.*

LIFE OF SAMUEL JOHNSON. By COLONEL F. GRANT.
"Colonel Grant has performed his task with diligence, sound judgment, good taste, and accuracy."—*Illustrated London News.*

LIFE OF DARWIN. By G. T. BETTANY.
"Mr. G. T. Bettany's *Life of Darwin* is a sound and conscientious work."—*Saturday Review.*

LIFE OF CHARLOTTE BRONTË. By A. BIRRELL.
"Those who know much of Charlotte Brontë will learn more, and those who know nothing about her will find all that is best worth learning in Mr. Birrell's pleasant book."—*St. James' Gazette.*

LIFE OF THOMAS CARLYLE. By R. GARNETT, LL.D.
"This is an admirable book. Nothing could be more felicitous and fairer than the way in which he takes us through Carlyle's life and works."—*Pall Mall Gazette.*

London: WALTER SCOTT, LIMITED, 24 Warwick Lane.

GREAT WRITERS—continued.

LIFE OF ADAM SMITH. By R. B. HALDANE, M.P.
"Written with a perspicuity seldom exemplified when dealing with economic science."—*Scotsman.*

LIFE OF KEATS. By W. M. ROSSETTI.
"Valuable for the ample information which it contains."—*Cambridge Independent.*

LIFE OF SHELLEY. By WILLIAM SHARP.
"The criticisms . . . entitle this capital monograph to be ranked with the best biographies of Shelley."—*Westminster Review.*

LIFE OF SMOLLETT. By DAVID HANNAY.
"A capable record of a writer who still remains one of the great masters of the English novel."—*Saturday Review.*

LIFE OF GOLDSMITH. By AUSTIN DOBSON.
"The story of his literary and social life in London, with all its humorous and pathetic vicissitudes, is here retold, as none could tell it better."—*Daily News.*

LIFE OF SCOTT. By PROFESSOR YONGE.
"This is a most enjoyable book."—*Aberdeen Free Press.*

LIFE OF BURNS. By PROFESSOR BLACKIE.
"The editor certainly made a hit when he persuaded Blackie to write about Burns."—*Pall Mall Gazette.*

LIFE OF VICTOR HUGO. By FRANK T. MARZIALS.
"Mr. Marzials's volume presents to us, in a more handy form than any English or even French handbook gives, the summary of what is known about the life of the great poet."—*Saturday Review.*

LIFE OF EMERSON. By RICHARD GARNETT, LL.D.
"No record of Emerson's life could be more desirable."—*Saturday Review.*

LIFE OF GOETHE. By JAMES SIME.
"Mr. James Sime's competence as a biographer of Goethe is beyond question."—*Manchester Guardian.*

LIFE OF CONGREVE. By EDMUND GOSSE.
"Mr. Gosse has written an admirable biography."—*Academy.*

LIFE OF BUNYAN. By CANON VENABLES.
"A most intelligent, appreciative, and valuable memoir."—*Scotsman.*

LIFE OF CRABBE. By T. E. KEBBEL.
"No English poet since Shakespeare has observed certain aspects of nature and of human life more closely."—*Athenæum.*

LIFE OF HEINE. By WILLIAM SHARP.
"An admirable monograph . . . more fully written up to the level of recent knowledge and criticism than any other English work."—*Scotsman.*

London: WALTER SCOTT, LIMITED, 24 Warwick Lane.

GREAT WRITERS—continued.

LIFE OF MILL. By W. L. COURTNEY.
"A most sympathetic and discriminating memoir."—*Glasgow Herald.*

LIFE OF SCHILLER. By HENRY W. NEVINSON.
"Presents the poet's life in a neatly rounded picture."—*Scotsman.*

LIFE OF CAPTAIN MARRYAT. By DAVID HANNAY.
"We have nothing but praise for the manner in which Mr. Hannay has done justice to him."—*Saturday Review.*

LIFE OF LESSING. By T. W. ROLLESTON.
"One of the best books of the series."—*Manchester Guardian.*

LIFE OF MILTON. By RICHARD GARNETT, LL.D.
"Has never been more charmingly or adequately told."—*Scottish Leader.*

LIFE OF BALZAC. By FREDERICK WEDMORE.
"Mr. Wedmore's monograph on the greatest of French writers of fiction, whose greatness is to be measured by comparison with his successors, is a piece of careful and critical composition, neat and nice in style."—*Daily News.*

LIFE OF GEORGE ELIOT. By OSCAR BROWNING.
"A book of the character of Mr. Browning's, to stand midway between the bulky work of Mr. Cross and the very slight sketch of Miss Blind, was much to be desired, and Mr. Browning has done his work with vivacity, and not without skill."—*Manchester Guardian.*

LIFE OF JANE AUSTEN. By GOLDWIN SMITH.
"Mr. Goldwin Smith has added another to the not inconsiderable roll of eminent men who have found their delight in Miss Austen. . . . His little book upon her, just published by Walter Scott, is certainly a fascinating book to those who already know her and love her well; and we have little doubt that it will prove also a fascinating book to those who have still to make her acquaintance."—*Spectator.*

LIFE OF BROWNING. By WILLIAM SHARP.
"This little volume is a model of excellent English, and in every respect it seems to us what a biography should be."—*Public Opinion.*

LIFE OF BYRON By HON. RODEN NOEL.
"The Hon. Roden Noel's volume on Byron is decidedly one of the most readable in the excellent 'Great Writers' series."—*Scottish Leader.*

LIFE OF HAWTHORNE. By MONCURE CONWAY.
"It is a delightful *causerie*—pleasant, genial talk about a most interesting man. Easy and conversational as the tone is throughout, no important fact is omitted, no valueless fact is recalled; and it is entirely exempt from platitude and conventionality."—*The Speaker.*

LIFE OF SCHOPENHAUER. By PROFESSOR WALLACE.
"We can speak very highly of this little book of Mr. Wallace's. It is, perhaps, excessively lenient in dealing with the man, and it cannot be said to be at all ferociously critical in dealing with the philosophy."—*Saturday Review.*

London: WALTER SCOTT, LIMITED, 24 Warwick Lane.

GREAT WRITERS—continued.

LIFE OF SHERIDAN. By LLOYD SANDERS.

"To say that Mr. Lloyd Sanders, in this little volume, has produced the best existing memoir of Sheridan, is really to award much fainter praise than the work deserves."—*Manchester Examiner.*

LIFE OF THACKERAY. By HERMAN MERIVALE and F. T. MARZIALS.

"The monograph just published is well worth reading, . . . and the book, with its excellent bibliography, is one which neither the student nor the general reader can well afford to miss."—*Pall Mall Gazette.*

LIFE OF CERVANTES. By H. E. WATTS.

"We can commend this book as a worthy addition to the useful series to which it belongs."—*London Daily Chronicle.*

LIFE OF VOLTAIRE. By FRANCIS ESPINASSE.

George Saintsbury, in *The Illustrated London News*, says:—"In this little volume the wayfaring man who has no time to devour libraries will find most things that it concerns him to know about Voltaire's actual life and work put very clearly, sufficiently, and accurately for the most part."

LIFE OF LEIGH HUNT. By COSMO MONKHOUSE.

"Mr. Monkhouse has brought together and skilfully set in order much widely scattered material . . . candid as well as sympathetic." — *The Athenæum.*

LIFE OF WHITTIER. By W. J. LINTON.

"Well written, and well worthy to stand with preceding volumes in the useful 'Great Writers' series."—*Black and White.*

LIBRARY EDITION OF "GREAT WRITERS," Demy 8vo, 2s. 6d.

London: WALTER SCOTT, LIMITED, 24 Warwick Lane.

Crown 8vo, about 350 pp. each, Cloth Cover, 2s. 6d. per vol.
Half-polished Morocco, gilt top, 5s.

COUNT TOLSTOÏ'S WORKS.

The following Volumes are already issued—

A RUSSIAN PROPRIETOR.

THE COSSACKS.

IVAN ILYITCH, AND OTHER STORIES.

MY RELIGION.

LIFE.

MY CONFESSION.

CHILDHOOD, BOYHOOD, YOUTH.

THE PHYSIOLOGY OF WAR.

ANNA KARÉNINA 3s. 6d.

WHAT TO DO?

WAR AND PEACE. (4 VOLS.)

THE LONG EXILE, AND OTHER STORIES FOR CHILDREN.

SEVASTOPOL.

THE KREUTZER SONATA, AND FAMILY HAPPINESS.

Uniform with the above.

IMPRESSIONS OF RUSSIA.

BY DR. GEORG BRANDES.

London: WALTER SCOTT, LIMITED, 24 Warwick Lane.

NEW ENGLAND LIBRARY.

CLOTH, GILT TOP, 2s. EACH.

Contains the following Works—

NATHANIEL HAWTHORNE.

1. THE HOUSE OF THE SEVEN GABLES.
2. THE SCARLET LETTER.
3. MOSSES FROM AN OLD MANSE.
4. THE NEW ADAM AND EVE.
5. TWICE-TOLD TALES.
6. LEGENDS OF THE PROVINCE HOUSE.
7. THE SNOW IMAGE.
8. OUR OLD HOME.
9. TANGLEWOOD TALES.
10. THE BLITHEDALE ROMANCE.
11. TRUE STORIES FROM HISTORY AND BIOGRAPHY.
12. A WONDER-BOOK FOR GIRLS AND BOYS.

A. S. HARDY.

13. BUT YET A WOMAN.

THEO. WINTHROP.

14. CECIL DREEME.
15. JOHN BRENT.
16. EDWIN BROTHERTOFT.
17. CANOE AND SADDLE.

O. W. HOLMES.

18. AUTOCRAT OF THE BREAKFAST-TABLE.
19. PROFESSOR AT THE BREAKFAST-TABLE.
20. POET AT THE BREAKFAST-TABLE.
21. ELSIE VENNER.
22. A MORTAL ANTIPATHY.

WASHINGTON IRVING.

23. THE SKETCH BOOK.
24. CHRISTMAS.

In ordering, it is sufficient to note the numbers to the above titles.

London: WALTER SCOTT, LIMITED, 24 Warwick Lane.

VAIN FORTUNE. By GEORGE MOORE. With Eleven Illustrations by MAURICE GREIFFENHAGEN.

MODERN PAINTING. A Volume of Essays. By GEORGE MOORE.

PEER GYNT: A DRAMATIC POEM. By HENRIK IBSEN. Translated by WILLIAM and CHARLES ARCHER.

AMONG THE CAMPS; OR, YOUNG PEOPLE'S STORIES OF THE WAR. By THOMAS NELSON PAGE. (Illustrated.)

THE MUSIC OF THE POETS: A MUSICIANS' BIRTHDAY BOOK. Edited by ELEONORE D'ESTERRE KEELING.

THE GERM-PLASM: A THEORY OF HEREDITY. By AUGUST WEISMANN, Professor in the University of Freiburg-in-Breisgau.

London: WALTER SCOTT, LIMITED, 24 Warwick Lane.

BOOKS AT 3/6.

THE INSPECTOR-GENERAL. A Russian Comedy, by NIKOLAI V. GOGOL. Translated by ARTHUR A. SYKES.

THE CAREER OF A NIHILIST. By STEPNIAK.

ANNA KARÉNINA. By COUNT TOLSTOÏ. Translated by N. H. DOLE.

CRIME AND PUNISHMENT. By F. DOSTOIEFFSKY.

A DRAMA IN MUSLIN. By GEORGE MOORE.

THE MUMMER'S WIFE. By GEORGE MOORE.

A MODERN LOVER. By GEORGE MOORE.

THE NEW BORDER TALES. By SIR GEORGE DOUGLAS, BART. (Illustrated.)

FROM AUSTRALIA AND JAPAN. A collection of Short Stories. By A. M. (Illustrated.)

FOR LUST OF GOLD: A NARRATIVE OF ADVENTURE. By AARON WATSON. (Illustrated.)

SCOTTISH FAIRY AND FOLK TALES. By SIR GEORGE DOUGLAS, BART. (Illustrated.)

ENGLISH FAIRY AND FOLK TALES. Edited by E. SIDNEY HARTLAND. (Illustrated.)

IRISH FAIRY AND FOLK TALES. Edited and Selected by W. B. YEATS. (Illustrated.)

DRAMATIC ESSAYS. Edited by WILLIAM ARCHER and ROBERT W. LOWE. 3 Vols.
The First Series contains the criticisms of LEIGH HUNT.
The Second Series contains the criticisms of WILLIAM HAZLITT.
The Third Series contains hitherto uncollected criticisms by JOHN FORSTER, GEORGE HENRY LEWES, and others.

IBSEN'S PROSE DRAMAS—Edited by WM. ARCHER.
VOL. I. "A DOLL'S HOUSE," "THE LEAGUE OF YOUTH," and "THE PILLARS OF SOCIETY."
VOL. II. "GHOSTS," "AN ENEMY OF THE PEOPLE," and "THE WILD DUCK." With an Introductory Note.
VOL. III. "LADY INGER OF ÖSTRÅT," "THE VIKINGS AT HELGELAND," "THE PRETENDERS."
VOL. IV. "EMPEROR AND GALILEAN." With an Introductory Note by WILLIAM ARCHER.
VOL. V. "ROSMERSHOLM," "THE LADY FROM THE SEA," "HEDDA GABLER."

London: WALTER SCOTT, LIMITED, 24 Warwick Lane.

THE CANTERBURY POETS.

EDITED BY WILLIAM SHARP. IN 1/- MONTHLY VOLUMES.

| Cloth, Red Edges | - | 1s. | Red Roan, Gilt Edges, 2s. 6d. |
| Cloth, Uncut Edges | - | 1s. | Pad. Morocco, Gilt Edges, 5s. |

THE CHRISTIAN YEAR ....By the Rev. John Keble.
COLERIDGE ....Edited by Joseph Skipsey.
LONGFELLOW ....Edited by Eva Hope.
CAMPBELL..Edited by John Hogben.
SHELLEY...Edited by Joseph Skipsey.
WORDSWORTH ....Edited by A. J. Symington.
BLAKE ....Edited by Joseph Skipsey.
WHITTIER ....Edited by Eva Hope.
POE ....Edited by Joseph Skipsey.
CHATTERTON ....Edited by John Richmond.
BURNS. Poems ....Edited by Joseph Skipsey.
BURNS. Songs ....Edited by Joseph Skipsey.
MARLOWE ....Edited by Percy E. Pinkerton.
KEATS...Edited by John Hogben.
HERBERT..Edited by Ernest Rhys.
HUGO ....Translated by Dean Carrington.
COWPER...Edited by Eva Hope.
SHAKESPEARE'S POEMS, Etc. ....Edited by William Sharp.
EMERSON ....Edited by Walter Lewin.
SONNETS OF THIS CENTURY ....Edited by William Sharp.
WHITMAN ....Edited by Ernest Rhys.
SCOTT. Marmion, etc. ....Edited by William Sharp.
SCOTT. Lady of the Lake, etc. ....Edited by William Sharp.
PRAED ....Edited by Frederick Cooper.
HOGG ....Edited by his Daughter, Mrs. Garden.
GOLDSMITH ....Edited by William Tirebuck.
LOVE LETTERS, Etc......................................By Eric Mackay.
SPENSER..Edited by Hon. Roden Noel.
CHILDREN OF THE POETS ....Edited by Eric S. Robertson.
JONSON ....Edited by J. Addington Symonds.
BYRON (2 Vols.)..................................Edited by Mathilde Blind.
THE SONNETS OF EUROPE ....Edited by S. Waddington.
RAMSAY ....Edited by J. Logie Robertson.
DOBELL ....Edited by Mrs. Dobell

London: WALTER SCOTT, LIMITED, 24 Warwick Lane.

THE CANTERBURY POETS—continued.

DAYS OF THE YEAR .... With Introduction by William Sha[rp]
POPE .... Edited by John Hogb[en]
HEINE .... Edited by Mrs. Kroe[ker]
BEAUMONT AND FLETCHER .... Edited by John S. Fletch[er]
BOWLES, LAMB, &c. .... Edited by William Tirebu[ck]
EARLY ENGLISH POETRY .... Edited by H. Macaulay Fitzgibb[on]
SEA MUSIC .... Edited by Mrs Sha[rp]
HERRICK .... Edited by Ernest Rh[ys]
BALLADES AND RONDEAUS .... Edited by J. Gleeson Whi[te]
IRISH MINSTRELSY .... Edited by H. Halliday Sparli[ng]
MILTON'S PARADISE LOST ...... Edited by J. Bradshaw, M.A., LL[.D.]
JACOBITE BALLADS .... Edited by G. S. Macquo[id]
AUSTRALIAN BALLADS .... Edited by D. B. W. Sladen, B.[A.]
MOORE .... Edited by John Dorri[an]
BORDER BALLADS .... Edited by Graham R. Toms[on]
SONG-TIDE .... By Philip Bourke Marst[on]
ODES OF HORACE .... Translations by Sir Stephen de Vere,
OSSIAN .... Edited by George Eyre-To[dd]
ELFIN MUSIC .... Edited by Arthur Edward Wai[te]
SOUTHEY .... Edited by Sidney R. Thomps[on]
CHAUCER .... Edited by Frederick Noël Pat[on]
POEMS OF WILD LIFE .... Edited by Charles G. D. Roberts, M.[A.]
PARADISE REGAINED .... Edited by J. Bradshaw, M.A., LL[.D.]
CRABBE .... Edited by E. Lamplou[gh]
DORA GREENWELL .... Edited by William Dorli[ng]
FAUST .... Edited by Elizabeth Craigm[yle]
AMERICAN SONNETS .... Edited by William Sha[rp]
LANDOR'S POEMS .... Edited by Ernest Radfo[rd]
GREEK ANTHOLOGY .... Edited by Graham R. Toms[on]
HUNT AND HOOD .... Edited by J. Harwood Pantin[g]
HUMOROUS POEMS .... Edited by Ralph H. Cai[ne]
LYTTON'S PLAYS .... Edited by R. Farquharson Sha[rp]
GREAT ODES .... Edited by William Sha[rp]
MEREDITH'S POEMS .... Edited by M. Betham-Edwar[ds]
PAINTER-POETS .... Edited by Kineton Park[es]
WOMEN POETS .... Edited by Mrs. Sha[rp]
LOVE LYRICS .... Edited by Percy Hulbur[t]
AMERICAN HUMOROUS VERSE .... Edited by James Ba[rr]
MINOR SCOTCH LYRICS .... Edited by Sir George Dougl[as]
CAVALIER LYRISTS .... Edited by Will H. Dirc[ks]
GERMAN BALLADS .... Edited by Elizabeth Craigmy[le]
SONGS OF BERANGER .... Translated by William Toynbe[e]
HON. RODEN NOEL'S POEMS. With an Introduction by R. Buchana[n]
SONGS OF FREEDOM. Selected, with an Introduction, by H. S. Sa[lt]
CANADIAN POEMS AND LAYS .... Edited by W. D. Lighthall, M.[A.]
CONTEMPORARY SCOTTISH VERSE. Edited by Sir Geo. Dougl[as]

www.ingramcontent.com/pod-product-compliance
Lightning Source LLC
Chambersburg PA
CBHW031738230426
43669CB00007B/387